Discovery

# Sharkopedia

*With an introduction by Andy Dehart,*
*Marine Biologist and "Shark Week" expert*

**SHARK WEEK**

# THE COMPLETE GUIDE TO EVERYTHING SHARK

# LIBERTY
## STREET

Published by Liberty Street, an imprint of Time Inc. Books, a division of Meredith Corporation
225 Liberty Street
New York, NY 10281

LIBERTY STREET is a trademark of Time Inc.

**ISBN: 978-1-60320-964-9**

**6 QGV 18**

**10 9 8 7 6**

We welcome your comments and suggestions about Time Inc. Books. Please write to us at:
Time Inc. Books, Attention: Book Editors,
P.O. Box 62310, Tampa, FL 33662-2310
(800) 765-6400

timeincbooks.com

Time Inc. Books products may be purchased for business or promotional use. For information on bulk purchases, please contact Christi Crowley in the Special Sales Department at (845) 895-9858.

**Produced by**

**President and Editorial Director:** Susan Knopf
**Project Manager and Writer:** Lori Stein
**Advisor:** Andy Dehart, Marine Biologist
**Designed by:** Andrij Borys Associates, LLC
**Senior Designers:** Andrij Borys, Brian Greenberg
**Associate Designers:** Mia Balaquiot, Iwona Usakiewicz
**Special Thanks:** Tracy Collins, Cady Burnes, Sara Shaffer, Ethan Borys, Leslie Garisto, and James S. Harrison.

## ABOUT THIS BOOK

*Sharkopedia* is your guide to the fascinating world of sharks. Sharks have been swimming in the world's oceans since before dinosaurs roamed the earth, and while dinosaurs died out sharks have survived. In fact, they're masters of survival, and they have developed many special features as they have evolved and adapted. They are intelligent, they are expert hunters, and they have exceptional senses.

This book is filled with information about the world's most infamous sharks, including great white, bull, and tiger sharks. It explains the shark's unique tooth replacement system that allows sharks to chomp through thousands of teeth in a lifetime, which are the two fastest-swimming sharks, how some sharks get their teeth cleaned, and why tiger sharks are known as "garbage guts." The book shows the different ways sharks breathe, which shark pups (babies) grow in egg cases known as mermaid's purses, and how dermal denticles help sharks zip through the water.

*Sharkopedia* also takes a look at the ways in which sharks are misunderstood. Yes, sharks sometimes do bite people, but not as often as most people think. Sharks don't really like people—although they sometimes take a test bite of something moving in the water to see if it's good to eat, and their strong jaws and sharp teeth can do a lot of damage. Sharks are in greater danger from people than they are dangerous to people. Overfishing has contributed to declining populations in some shark species, and this book talks about shark conservation efforts and offers suggestions for things people can do to help these amazing creatures survive. Shark expert Andy Dehart, a marine biologist who works with and cares deeply about sharks, has provided an introduction and special contributions throughout the book under the heading "Andy Says."

You can dip into any one of the close-up portraits of the different shark species and the fact-filled special topics sections to learn a lot of good stuff, but first check out Shark Orders and The Body of the Beast on the following pages for information that will help as you read the rest of the book.

# Contents

# Introduction

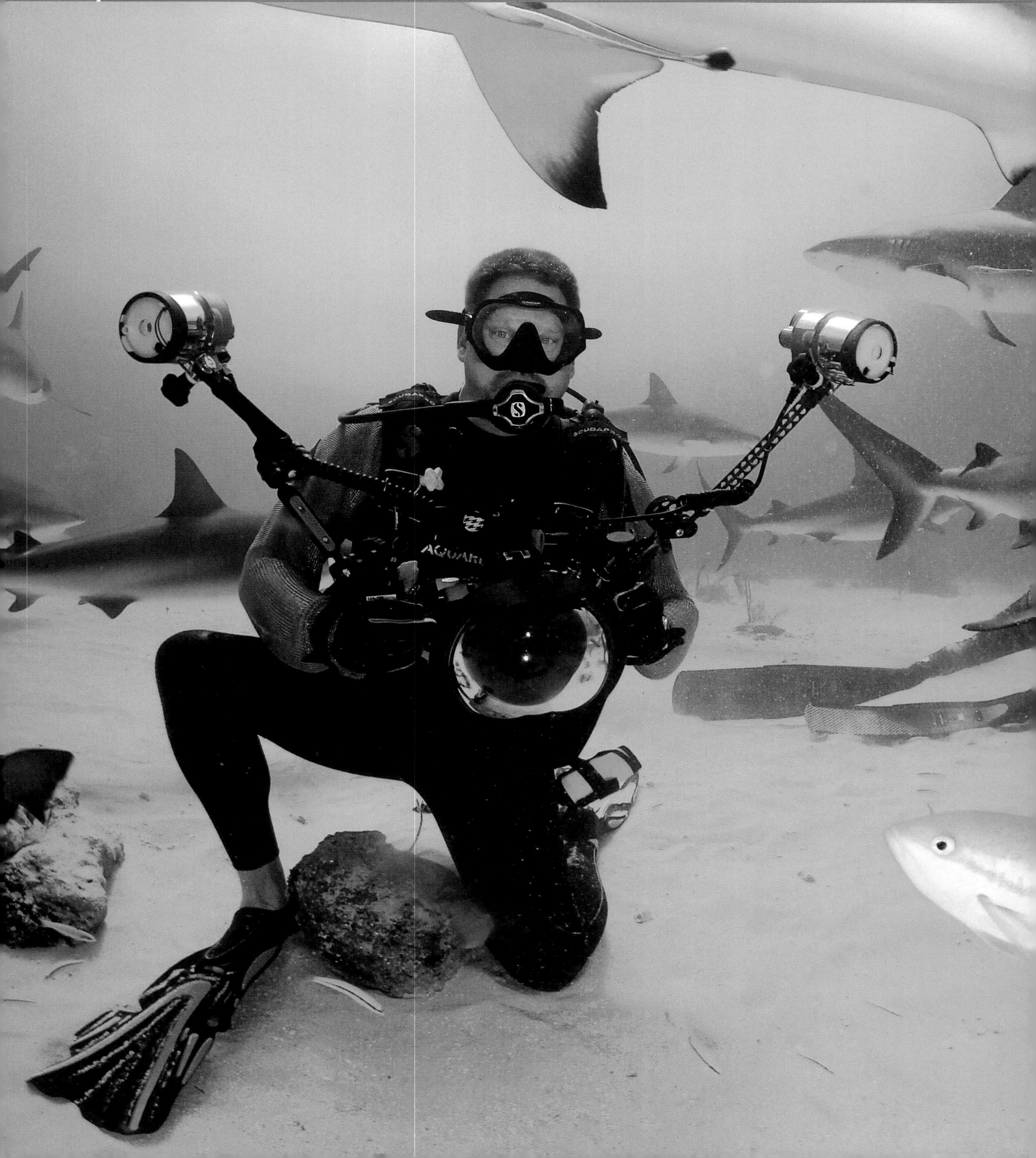

I have been fascinated by sharks since the first time I swam with them when I was five while snorkeling with my dad. I turned that fascination into a career; I have worked with sharks for over 20 years. As a kid, I pored through books like this one until the bindings fell off to learn all that I could about sharks. It has been a pleasure to be a part of this project in the hope that the next generation of marine biologists is doing the same.

New advances in technology have allowed scientists to learn a great deal about sharks. One thing that is abundantly clear is that sharks are not the mindless monsters of the deep that they were once thought to be. On very rare occasions, sharks have bitten humans, sometimes with tragic results. Around the globe, there are fewer than 100 shark bites per year. Of these, on average six are fatal. Most of these are cases of mistaken identity as there is not a single shark species that has humans as part of its diet.

The same cannot be said for sharks as part of the human diet. More than 70 million sharks are killed each year, primarily for their fins, which are used in shark fin soup. A bowl of this soup can sell for as much as $200. The value of these fins is leading to incredible fishing pressure on these amazing animals. Although there are many species of sharks that have healthy populations, there are others that are in rapid decline. As an example, the scalloped hammerhead population in the Atlantic has declined by over 90 percent in the last 20 years.

Through my work at public aquariums and in shows for Discovery Channel's "Shark Week," I have had numerous face-to-face encounters with many species of sharks, including some of the sharks known to be most dangerous. Through all of these experiences I have seen firsthand that sharks certainly are not monsters and definitely not mindless. In fact, they are far smarter than most people realize and are able to learn behaviors such as swimming to targets for food and learning to roll over for veterinary procedures. Being able to work with the same sharks year after year and observing each individual shark's unique behaviors is the best part of my career.

Whether you are fascinated by sharks or fearful of them, the fact remains that they need our help to survive. This book identifies many organizations committed to helping save sharks. I encourage you to get involved to help these amazing animals for their survival and for the role they play in the health of the world's oceans.

*Andy Dehart, Marine Biologist*
*and "Shark Week" expert*

# Shark Parts

Sharks don't all look the same; they come in many sizes, shapes, and colors. They don't behave the same: Some are gentle and slow-moving; some are fierce and fast. They don't all live in the same place or eat the same food. So what does a fish need to be called a shark?

**Cartilage**   Sharks don't have bones. Instead, their skeletons are made of a tough, flexible material called cartilage. People have cartilage in their bodies, too—the flexible parts of ears and noses are made of cartilage. Cartilage allows sharks to twist their bodies into small spaces so that they can catch prey more easily.

**Upper and lower jaws**   Sharks have powerful jaws that are not fused to their heads. This allows them to thrust their jaws forward when hunting. Their upper and lower jaws are hinged together in a way that allows them to catch their prey efficiently.

**Fins**   Sharks have one or two dorsal fins, a large caudal (tail) fin, and a pectoral fin. Sharks use their fins to move through the water. Some sharks have huge, well-developed fins; some have smaller ones.

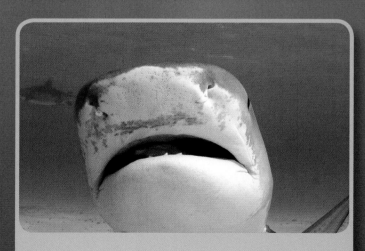

**Nostrils under their heads**   Sharks don't breathe through their nostrils the way people do. Instead, they take water into their nostrils as they swim and the water passes over sensory organs that pick up scents from the water. These sensory organs are responsible for a shark's keen sense of smell.

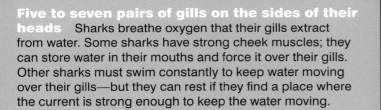

**Five to seven pairs of gills on the sides of their heads**   Sharks breathe oxygen that their gills extract from water. Some sharks have strong cheek muscles; they can store water in their mouths and force it over their gills. Other sharks must swim constantly to keep water moving over their gills—but they can rest if they find a place where the current is strong enough to keep the water moving.

**Special features**   Sharks have extra senses that make them superior hunters. Ampullae of Lorenzini are tiny ducts that sense electrical impulses that all living things emit. Lateral lines and pit organs are also sense organs. Sharks have rows of teeth and a unique tooth-replacement system: When a tooth from a front row falls out, one from the row behind moves up to take its place.

A wobbegong is flat, brown, and lives on the ocean floor.

A blue shark is indigo blue, with a cylindrical body, and swims in open ocean.

## SHARK DIVERSITY

Sharks share many similar features, but that doesn't stop them from looking and behaving very differently.

**Size**   Sharks can be as small as a 7-inch dwarf lanternshark and as big as a 40-foot whale shark.

**Color**   Most sharks come in shades of gray and brown. But the goblin shark is bright pink, makos are metallic blue, and lemon sharks are sandy yellow. Many sharks, such as the chain catshark, the puffadder shyshark, and the zebra shark, have bright patterns in yellow, orange, pink, and green.

**Shape**   Some sharks, such as great whites and salmon sharks, are long with round bodies. Others, including wobbegongs and angelsharks, look flat. Frilled sharks and some carpetsharks look more like snakes or eels than like most other sharks. Some, like horn sharks, goblin sharks, and sawsharks, have odd ridges, beaks, and bumps on their heads.

# The Body of the Beast

Different sharks have different bodies but most have the same features. Here is how those features are arranged on a Caribbean reef shark, shown below.

Caudal fin

Anal fin

Pelvic fin

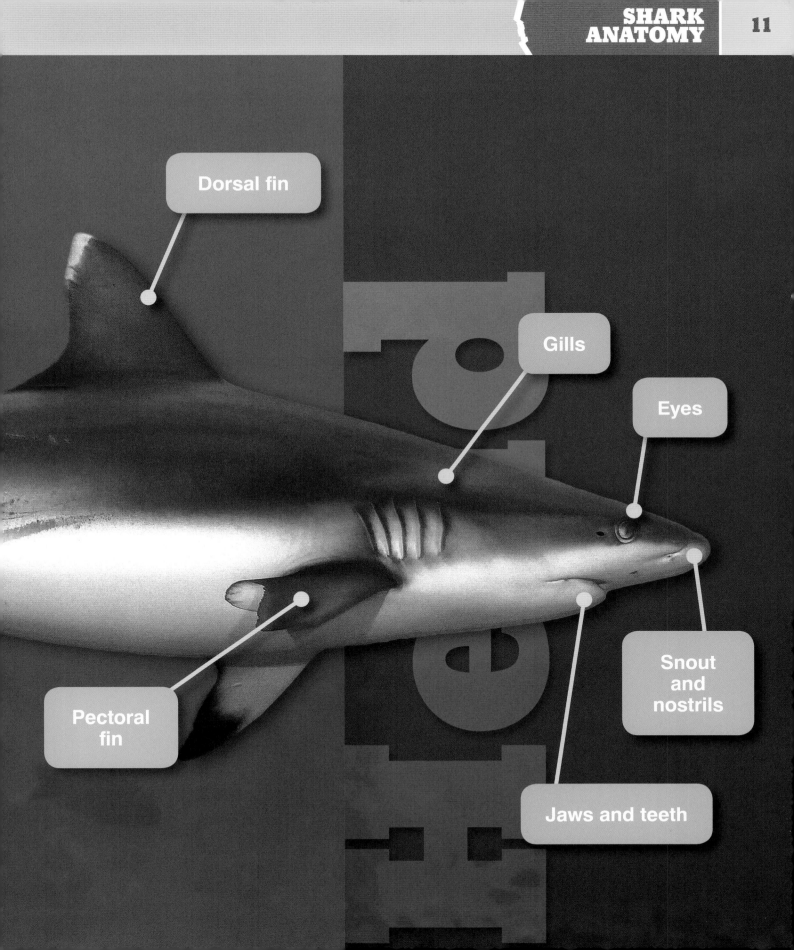

Dorsal fin

Gills

Eyes

Pectoral
fin

Snout
and
nostrils

Jaws and teeth

# Cartilage: No Bones

Shark skeletons are made only of cartilage; they don't have any bones in their bodies. The human skeleton is mostly made from bones that are connected to one another with cartilage, which is thick and flexible. This cartilage allows people to bend their knees and elbows. Human noses and ears are flexible, too—they contain cartilage.

## CARTILAGINOUS FISH

Sharks are not the only fish that have cartilage instead of bone. Skates, rays, and chimeras are also members of the group called cartilaginous fish. The fish in this group all have gills and skin that are somewhat different from those of other fish: Their gills are exposed, and their skin is covered with toothy projections called dermal denticles instead of scales. This kind of skeleton has been around for about 400 million years, and cartilaginous fish can live for 50 to 100 years or more—so obviously, this system helps them to survive.

Smaller sharks like this catshark can slide over rough places with their boneless bodies.

## CARTILAGE IS GOOD FOR SHARKS

The no-bones system works very well for sharks. They can twist and turn their bodies and get into tight places when they are chasing prey. Cartilage is lighter than bone, so sharks' bodies are lighter than they would be if they were filled with bones. This makes it easier for them to stay afloat, and they need less energy to push their bodies through the water.

Some of the features that all sharks have are fins, gills, skin covered with small toothy projections called dermal denticles, and cartilage.

## CALCIFICATION

Calcium crystals sometimes mix with cartilage and make it hard. In certain parts of the sharks, such as the jaws and fins, calcification makes the cartilage stronger. An older shark, with calcified jaws, has a stronger bite than a young shark whose jaws are still soft.

## RED BLOOD CELLS

Red blood cells are usually manufactured in the marrow (the center part) of bones. How do animals that don't have bones, like sharks, make the red blood cells their bodies need? In sharks, these are made by the spleen or the thymus gland. Some sharks also have a body part called Leydig's organ that makes the cells. Red blood cells carry oxygen and also help animals fight disease (white blood cells play an even larger role in fighting disease). It takes less time for the disease-fighting red blood cells to reach the bloodstream in a shark's system than it does for red blood cells that are made in bone marrow. Scientists think this might be one of the reasons that sharks don't get diseases as often as some other animals.

Lemon sharks twist and turn as they seek prey in a feeding frenzy, which occurs when many sharks are attracted to prey at the same time.

Sharks can twist their bodies to get closer to prey.

# Skin: Coveralls

Shark skin, just like human skin, is more than a covering for the skeleton and organs. Shark skin is covered in toothlike projections called dermal denticles that make it hard to pierce. This is especially useful for small sharks, as it can prevent them from being eaten by bigger fish. The skin of some sharks has colors and patterns—spots, dots, blotches, and stripes—which camouflage the shark so predators can't see it. Shark skin also contains sensory nerve cells that alert the shark to changes in water temperature and the presence of prey and predators.

Whale sharks have the thickest skin of any animal.

## THICK SKINS

Most sharks have thick skin. The thickest animal skin in the world is on whale sharks—it's up to 3½ inches thick. Shark skin has two layers. The top layer is made up of dead cells from the bottom layer, which it protects. The bottom layer is composed of muscles, sensory nerve cells, and blood vessels.

## THE DENTICLE ADVANTAGE

Sharks have denticles all over their bodies. These toothy projections start in the lower level of the skin and pop up through the top layer. Each denticle is covered in enamel, which is the same hard coating found on human and shark teeth. Underneath the enamel is a space with nerve and blood cells. Denticles fall off throughout the shark's life, and more grow back.

### WORD!
Denticle means "small tooth."

Great white shark denticles are gray on the top of the body and white on the underbelly, matching the shark's skin color.

## FAST FACT

Some sharks with solid-colored bodies try to gain the advantage of countershading by getting suntans. Young scalloped hammerheads have been observed in Hawaii swimming just below surface so that the tops of their bodies become darker.

## BLENDING IN

The color of a shark's skin helps it blend into its surroundings so predators can't easily see it and so it can sneak up on prey (photos on the top row, below). Some sharks have skin that is countershaded, or dark on top and light underneath (photos on the bottom row). This makes them less easily spotted from a distance and harder to detect from below. as their light-colored bellies blend in with the sunlight and sky.

## DID YOU KNOW?

Denticles feel smooth when stroked from front to back, and rough the other way. They face to the back, away from the direction that sharks swim, which reduces drag and friction with the water and increases speed.

*Zebra shark*

*Chain catshark*

*Lemon shark*

*Great white shark*

Spiny dogfish scales, magnified

# Muscles and Fins

Swimming is the most constant activity in a shark's life. All sharks are equipped with a complicated set of muscles and fins to move them through the water.

## TAILS FOR SPEED

A shark's tail helps it go faster. Slow-moving sharks have weak tail muscles, but some sharks—like salmon sharks and makos—have strong muscles and their tails are like propellers that help them to zip through the water.

## FINS FOR LIFT, STABILITY, AND MANEUVERING

The size and strength of each fin varies from species to species, but all sharks have pectoral fins on each side of the body for lift, dorsal fins on the back for stability, and caudal fins on the tail that move them forward.

## WORD!

A keel is like a fin on the bottom of a sailboat; it keeps the boat from tipping over.

*Whitetip reef shark*

## MUSCLES FOR MOVEMENT

Sharks have muscles along their flanks, arranged in zigzag blocks. Each block overlaps a vertebra in the shark's spinal column. As the shark's muscles contract, the vertebrae are pulled closer to each other, which bends the spine. The spine moves back and forth in an S-shaped motion to move the shark forward and push the water back.

**Oceanic whitetip sharks** use their huge, oarlike fins as paddles.

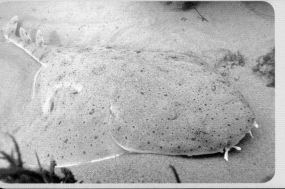

**Angelsharks** have strong muscles in their fins; they use them to bury themselves in the mud and sand of the ocean to hide themselves.

**Epaulette sharks** have fins that look like paddles they move back and forth along the ocean floor.

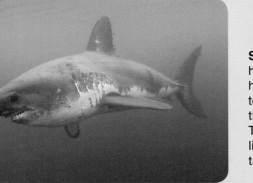

**Salmon sharks** have tails that are huge compared to the size of their bodies. They have a keel-like fin on their tails for balance.

Sharks breathe by using their gills to extract oxygen from the water around them. Most sharks have five sets of gills, but some have six or seven. Shark gills vary in size—basking sharks have huge gills that surround the head almost completely, and smoothhound sharks have smaller gills.

*Nurse shark*

*Tiger shark*

## DIFFERENT WAYS OF BREATHING

In order for gills to work, water has to pass over them. Sharks have a few ways of getting water to pass over their gills. Some sharks, usually those who don't swim a lot, have strong cheek muscles. They can hold water in their cheeks and then pump the water over their gills. These sharks, including wobbegongs, angelsharks, and nurse sharks, can rest on the ocean floor for a long time without swimming. This process is called buccal (cheek) breathing.

Sharks that don't have strong cheek muscles have to keep swimming to get water to pass over their gills. This is called ram ventilation because they have to push, or ram, their gills through water. Sometimes these sharks can find a place where currents are very strong and rest for a short time while the current moves water over their gills. Most big sharks, like great whites, makos, bulls, and tigers, are ram ventilators.

## HOW GILLS WORK

Blood flows through capillaries— small blood vessels—in shark gills. Since there is less oxygen in the blood moving inside the gills than there is dissolved oxygen in the water, the oxygen pushes into the blood across the thin membrane of the gills to equalize the number of molecules of oxygen. This is known as osmosis.

Great white sharks
must keep swimming
in order to breathe.

## OSMOREGULATION

Gills have another purpose besides
moving oxygen into a shark's bloodstream.
The amount of salt in a shark's body
is also regulated by gills. Most sharks live
in a salt water environment. They need
a salty compound, called urea, to maintain
a balance between the salt in the water
and in their bodies. If they build up too
much urea, they can push it out through
their gills, as well as through their skin.

Scientists estimate that there are nearly 500 kinds of sharks swimming in oceans around the world. This doesn't refer to the number of individual sharks, but rather to the number of "named sharks."

What is a named shark? A Swedish scientist named Carl Linnaeus devised a system for sorting and naming all the living things on the planet nearly 300 years ago. Linnaeus used Latin and Greek names because those were the languages of scientific study, and they are still used today.

Sand tiger sharks are also called grey nurse sharks and raggedtooth sharks.

Most people don't use sharks' full scientific names when talking about them. Instead, they use common names. For example, we call *Carcharias taurus* (Kahr-KAHR-ee-us TAW-russ) by its common name, the sand tiger shark, which is easier to pronounce and to remember. The challenge is that common names change from region to region—the sand tiger shark is the grey nurse shark in Australia and the raggedtooth shark in South Africa. But every animal has only one scientific name.

## NOMENCLATURE KNOW-HOW

It is easy to remember this seemingly complicated ranking system from the broadest category (kingdom) to the most specific (species) with an easy memory aid, called a mnemonic (nih-MAHN-ick):

**Kangaroos paddle canoes out from Ghana slowly.**

| | | |
|---|---|---|
| **K**angaroos ➡ ➡ ➡ | **K**ingdom |
| **P**addle ➡ ➡ ➡ ➡ | **P**hylum |
| **C**anoes ➡ ➡ ➡ ➡ | **C**lass |
| **O**ut ➡ ➡ ➡ ➡ | **O**rder |
| **F**rom ➡ ➡ ➡ ➡ | **F**amily |
| **G**hana ➡ ➡ ➡ ➡ | **G**enus |
| **S**lowly ➡ ➡ ➡ ➡ | **S**pecies |

Tiger sharks are nicknamed "garbage guts."

## NICKNAMES

In addition to their official common names, many sharks have nicknames. The white shark is also called the great white shark, the white pointer shark, the maneater shark, and white death. Bull sharks are nicknamed Zambis in Africa and are sometimes called shovelnoses because they hit their prey with their big snouts. Tiger sharks are called "garbage guts" because they'll eat anything.

A long time ago, scientists devised a system for naming all the creatures in the world, including sharks. By learning these names, we can know exactly which one we're talking about.

# SCIENTIFIC NAMING SYSTEM FOR ANIMALS

**Kingdom**

There are three categories of kingdom: animal, plant, and mineral.

Sharks are members of the animal kingdom.

*Plant*

**Phylum (FYE-lumm)** A division of a kingdom.

In the animal kingdom, there are two divisions: animals with backbones (called vertebrates) and animals without backbones (called invertebrates).

Sharks don't have bones, but they do have a backbone—it is made of cartilage, the same thing that human ears and noses are made of.

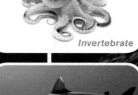
*Invertebrate*

**Class** Each phylum is divided into classes.

Classes include birds, fish, mammals, insects, and amphibians.

Sharks are in the fish class.

*Shark*

**Order** Orders are ways to organize and sort members of a class that share common features.

Sharks are organized into eight orders.

Great white sharks and thresher sharks are both part of the Mackerel Shark Order.

*Thresher shark*

Within an order, members with even more similarities are grouped together into a **family**.

There are 35 families of sharks altogether, including five families in the Mackerel Shark Order.

Great white sharks are in the Lamnidae Family. Thresher sharks are in the Alopiidae Family.

*Great white shark*

**Genus (JEAN-uss)** Family members with even more things in common are members of the same genus.

There are 105 different genera (JEH-nuh-rah, plural of "genus") of sharks, some with only one named shark in it and some with dozens of similar sharks.

The great white is the only shark in its genus. There are three thresher sharks in the Thresher Genus, the common thresher, the bigeye thresher, and the pelagic thresher.

*Common thresher shark*

**Species** Within each genus, there are different species.

While members of a species may have many different names, they all have a great deal in common.

The shortfin mako shark is a species. Some members of the species might be bigger or smaller, darker or lighter—but they are all in the same species.

*Shortfin mako shark*

Sharks are divided into eight orders. The Groundshark Order is large, with 270 different species, and is covered in five different sections in this book.

## ANGELSHARKS

18 species in one family, including Pacific angelsharks, common angelsharks, and sand devils

## CARPETSHARKS

42 species in seven families, including bamboo sharks, epaulette sharks, wobbegongs, nurse sharks, whale sharks, and zebra sharks

## DOGFISH SHARKS

120 species in seven families, including spiny dogfish, lanternsharks, and sleeper sharks

## FRILLED SHARKS AND COWSHARKS

Six species in two families, including frilled sharks, sixgill sharks, and sevengill sharks

## HORN SHARKS AND BULLHEADS

Nine species in one family, including Port Jackson sharks, horn sharks, and crested bullheads

## MACKEREL SHARKS

15 species in seven families, including great white sharks, basking sharks, mako sharks, and thresher sharks

## SAWSHARKS

Ten species in one family, including longnose sawsharks, sixgill sawsharks, and African dwarf sawsharks

*Angelshark*

*Wobbegong shark*

*Spiny dogfish shark*

*Sixgill shark*

*Horn shark*

*Great white shark*

*Sawshark*

Catshark

Hammerhead shark

Leopard shark

Tiger shark

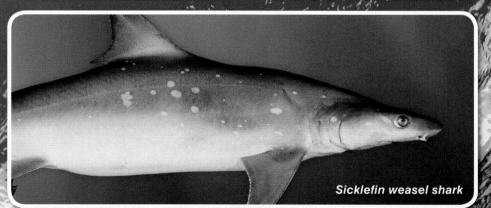
Sicklefin weasel shark

# GROUNDSHARKS

## CATSHARKS

160 species in three families, including catsharks, finback catsharks, and false catsharks

## HAMMERHEAD SHARKS

Nine species in one family, including scalloped hammerhead, great hammerhead, and bonnethead sharks

## HOUNDSHARKS

47 species in two families, including smoothhounds, topesharks, and whiskery sharks

## REQUIEM SHARKS

54 species in one family, including bull sharks, tiger sharks, lemon sharks, and blue sharks

## WEASEL SHARKS

Eight species in one family, including Atlantic weasel, Australian weasel, and snaggletooth sharks

**These five groups of sharks have many features in common. There are many species in the Groundshark Order, and they are grouped into five different sections in this book.**

**18 SPECIES**

## ANGELSHARKS
### Squatinidae

African Angelshark
Angular Angelshark
Argentine Angelshark
Australian Angelshark
Chilean Angelshark
Clouded Angelshark
Common Angelshark
Eastern Angelshark
Hidden Angelshark
Japanese Angelshark
Ocelated Angelshark
Ornate Angelshark
Pacific Angelshark
Sand Devil
Sawback Angelshark
Smoothback Angelshark
Taiwan Angelshark
Western Angelshark

*Common angelshark*

# Angelsharks

Ith their almost flat bodies and small snouts, angelsharks look more like their relatives, rays, than like other sharks. They live on the ocean floor in temperate and cool waters. Many angelsharks have colors or markings on their skin that help them blend into their surroundings. Their pectoral fins have strong muscles and they use them to dig into sand and mud and bury themselves until only their eyes and the tops of their bodies are visible. They can stay that way for days. They breathe by taking water into their cheeks and blowing it over their gills, which is called buccal (cheek) breathing.

## Highlights

### ORDER

Angelsharks
*Squatiniformes*

### NAME

Angelsharks are named for the winglike fins on their bodies.

### SPECIES

There are 18 species in one family in the angelshark group.

### SIZE

Most are around 6 to 8 feet long and weigh about 75 pounds.

### HABITAT

They reside in cool temperate waters in most areas of the world.

# Sneaky Devils

Angelsharks are also known as sand devils, and they behave more like devils than angels. With skin colored or patterned to camouflage them, they bury themselves in the sand and mud of the ocean floor until they blend into the background. Then, when prey comes near, they attack, opening their powerful jaws and thrusting upward. What with the angelshark's strong jaws, sharp teeth, and the element of surprise, the nearby small fish, crustaceans, and mollusks that angelsharks eat don't have a chance of escaping.

## PACIFIC ANGELSHARKS

Pacific angelsharks live on the western coasts of North and South America. They have pale skin with red, brown, and gray markings to blend into the ocean floor in that area. Pacific angelsharks grow to about 5 feet and weigh up to 60 pounds. They feed on bony fish that are common in their habitat, such as croaker, hake, halibut, and sometimes shellfish. Although angelsharks spend most of their time on the ocean floor waiting for prey, they swim at night, looking for places where there is more food or where fish have not figured out how angelsharks ambush prey.

## HOMEBODIES

Angelsharks are usually homebodies, and many live in relatively small areas.

**Australian angelshark**
The southern coast of Australia

**Japanese angelshark**
The western Pacific, from Japan to the Philippines

## SURPRISE!

Angelsharks are ambush predators, which means that they hide and then surprise their prey. It takes about one-tenth of a second for an angelshark to pop up and snatch its prey.

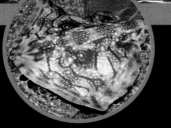

**Sand devils**
From the northern U.S. to northern South America

**Common angelshark**
North and Mediterranean seas, near Europe and Africa

**Rays**
are closely related to sharks, and look similar to angelsharks.

# Home Is Where the Food Is

Different sharks live in different habitats. Many sharks, like bullheads and smoothhounds, stay near coastlines where there is lots of food they like to eat. Other sharks, including threshers and hammerheads, roam the open sea—their habitat is huge, consisting of miles and miles of ocean that they swim through every day hunting for the bigger fish that live in the open waters.

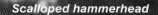

*Scalloped hammerhead*

The ocean floor is full of deep trenches and mountains called seamounts, some of which are hundreds of feet tall. Seamounts become habitats for many forms of marine life, including sharks that feast on creatures deposited there by tides.

*Lemon sharks*

A mangrove swamp is filled with vegetation, including mangrove shrubs. Tides fill the mangrove with water and bring in lots of small marine animals that are food for sharks.

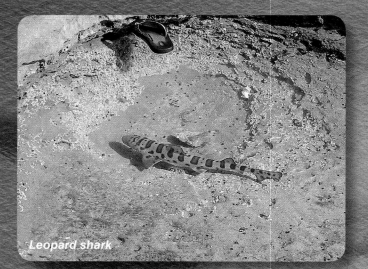

*Leopard shark*

Some sharks don't need deep water. Their habitats are tidal pools—shallow pools created by tides—and estuaries, where rivers meet seas. Currents bring food and sharks who live there avoid dealing with the harsh open ocean.

*Blacktip reef shark*

Kelp forests are underwater areas filled with kelp (seaweed). Sharks like to visit kelp forests to find the small fish that feed on the dense vegetation that grows there.

A habitat is the natural environment of a living creature. An ideal habitat will include everything the creature needs to survive: plenty of food, shelter from predators, the right amount of light, and a place to find a mate. When a creature finds an environment that has enough of what it needs to survive, it will stay, and that place is considered its habitat or home.

Great white shark

Angelshark

Broadnose sixgill shark

## OCEAN HABITATS

The **Sunlit Zone** of the ocean extends from the surface to a depth of up to 600 feet and is habitat to whale and basking sharks. The Sunlit Zone is home to a plentiful supply of plants, plankton, a variety of fish, sea lions, seals, sea turtles, and seabirds.

The Twilit Zone is below the Sunlit Zone and extends to a depth of about 3,000 feet below the surface. Some light filters down to this zone. Bottom dwellers such as sawsharks and angelsharks live there and eat shellfish that live on the ocean floor.

The deepest layer, from 3,000 feet down to the deepest parts of the ocean floor, is called **Permanent Midnight**. Some unusual-looking sharks live there and have special ways of finding food in the dark. Some deep-dwellers, like broadnose sixgill sharks, travel to the surface to feed at night.

Continental shelves are relatively shallow areas that are underwater extensions of the continental coastlines. Rivers that flow into the sea deposit all kinds of plant and animal life in these areas, which makes them rich feeding grounds for small fish. This attracts bigger fish, which eat the small fish, and it also attracts sharks looking for big and small fish.

Reefs form around piles of sand, rocks, or coral growths beneath the water's surface and they are home to many kinds of marine life. Reefs are places where all kinds of creatures, including sharks, interact and they are often compared to small cities—lively, crowded hubs of activity. The first to inhabit a reef are the smallest organisms, like plankton, which drift in on the tides. Fish come to eat the plankton, and then bigger fish come to eat the smaller fish. Sharks are an important part of the reef because they eat some of the bigger fish, which keeps those fish from devouring all the smaller fish at the reef.

## WORD!

An **ecosystem** is a combination of a physical habitat and its living population. The inhabitants of the ecosystem create a balance, with different groups living off one another so that one kind of creature does not take over. A lively reef is an ecosystem.

Coral may look like a rocky formation, but it's actually a living marine animal that, in most cases, has an external skeleton—which means that its bones are on the outside. Coral produces a hard substance made of a kind of calcium that binds coral animals to one another to form a coral reef. Coral is known for its gorgeous colors—all shades of white, pink, red, and yellow—and beautiful shapes.

Blacktip reef sharks regularly make visits to reefs.

## ANDY SAYS

The wrecks off North Carolina are one of the only places in the world to see sharks on an almost guaranteed basis without any baiting activities.
—*Andy Dehart, Marine Biologist*

## WRECKS: ARTIFICIAL REEFS

When ships sink at sea, they fall to the ocean floor. They attract marine life, because they provide structure and protection, which eventually form ecosystems. Small organisms like plankton and barnacles attach themselves to ship hulls and decks. Bigger fish, including sharks, join in. Sharks are such frequent visitors to shipwrecks that shipwrecks are sometimes called "shark motels."

## COLLARED CARPETSHARKS
### *Parascyllidae*
Barbelthroat Carpetshark
Collared Carpetshark
Elongate Carpetshark
Ginger Carpetshark
Necklace Carpetshark
Rusty Carpetshark
Saddled Carpetshark
Taiwan Saddled Carpetshark

## BLIND SHARKS
### *Brachaeluridae*
Blind Shark
Bluegrey Carpetshark

## WOBBEGONGS
### *Orectolobidae*
Banded or Gulf Wobbegong
Cobbler Wobbegong
Dwarf Spotted Wobbegong
Floral Banded Wobbegong
Indonesian Wobbegong
Japanese Wobbegong
Network Wobbegong
Northern Wobbegong
Ornate Wobbegong
Spotted Wobbegong
Tasselled Wobbegong
Western Wobbegong

## LONGTAILED CARPETSHARKS
### *Hemiscylliidae*
Arabian Carpetshark
Bluespotted Bamboo Shark
Brownbanded Bamboo Shark
Epaulette Shark
Gakei Bamboo Shark
Grey Bambooshark
Hasselt's Bamboo shark
Henry's Epaulette Shark
Hooded Carpetshark
Indonesian Speckled Carpetshark
Milne Bay Epaulette Shark
Papuan Epaulette Shark
Slender Bamboo Shark
Speckled Carpetshark
Whitespotted Bamboo Shark

## NURSE SHARKS
### *Ginglymostomatidae*
Nurse Shark
Shorttail Nurse Shark
Tawny Nurse Shark

## WHALE SHARK
### *Rhincodontidae*
Whale Shark

## ZEBRA SHARK
### *Stegostomatidae*
Zebra Shark

*Zebra shark*

# Carpetsharks

## Highlights

### ORDER

Carpetsharks
*Orectolobiformes*

### NAME

Carpetsharks are named for the elaborate patterns on their skin, which resemble patterned carpets.

### SPECIES

There are 42 species in the seven families of the Carpetshark Order.

### SIZE

The whale shark is the biggest in the Carpetshark Order and also the biggest fish in the world. It grows to more than 40 feet long and can weigh up to 70,000 pounds. The smallest carpetsharks, such as the barbelthroat and Taiwan saddle, are about 1 foot long.

### HABITAT

Most carpetsharks live in warm and tropical waters. The larger ones are found all over the world, but the smaller, less active ones live in the region between Asia and Australia.

Some carpetsharks are flat and live on the ocean floor. Some look more like snakes than sharks. Many are just a foot long, yet the biggest fish in the world is also a carpetshark. But carpetsharks have several features in common: two spineless dorsal fins, mouths in front of their eyes, and odd-looking sensory attachments called barbels that most often extend from their nostrils or jaws.

# Bamboos and Epaulettes

**A**lso known as longtailed carpetsharks, bamboo sharks have slender bodies and thick tails that are often as long as their bodies. This gives them a snakelike appearance, but their fins, gills, and teeth are all shark. They live in a relatively small area—in the Indian Ocean between Asia and Australia—and are usually found in shallow water, rocky underwater ledges, and intertidal pools. Most are small, measuring less than 3 feet long. Bamboo sharks are not aggressive. Their patterned skin helps them blend into their habitat so that both their prey and the fish that hunt them don't easily spot them.

Young bamboo sharks often have bolder colors that fade as they mature.

## PATTERNS

Carpetsharks have bold and colorful patterns on their skin. Different spots, dots, stripes, and colors help camouflage different carpetsharks.

**Whitespotted bamboo sharks** have brown bodies with darker brown stripes, dotted in white.

**Banded wobbegongs,** found in Australia, are golden brown with dark brown blotches and stripes.

## CAN SHARKS WALK?

Epaulette sharks have strong fins that look like paddles. When they move these paddles along the ocean bottom, they look as though they are walking rather than swimming. Epaulette sharks are sometimes called "walking sharks."

**Indonesian speckled carpetsharks**
have creamy light-colored skin with brown leopardlike spots.

**Whale sharks**
have lots of white spots and dots arranged all over their huge blue bodies.

**Bamboo sharks**
have long whiskerlike barbels that they use like feelers to rake along the ocean floor.

How did nurse sharks get their name? There are several theories. Is it because they resemble "nusee" sharks, an old name for catsharks? Is it because they make a sucking, or nursing, sound when they eat? No one knows for sure, but their scientific name, *Ginglymostoma cirratum*, refers to their curly mouths. Nurse sharks grow to about 9 feet long and live along the warmer parts of the coasts of North and South America and western Africa.

Nurse sharks favor small spaces. They can be found in coves and reefs and often squeeze their bodies into spaces that don't seem big enough for them. They swim actively during the night, and often return to the same place at daylight.

## DON'T PUCKER UP

Some divers kiss nurse sharks on the lips, but it's a risky endeavor. One diver surprised a sleeping nurse shark by waking it up with a kiss—and he was bitten on his lips. The diver survived, but is unlikely to pucker up with a sleeping nurse shark again.

### ANDY SAYS

Nurse sharks are responsible for a number of bites to humans but in almost every case a diver or snorkeler had harassed the animal, such as trying to pull it out of a cave while it is resting. So the lesson is, let sleeping sharks lie.
—Andy Dehart, Marine Biologist

How do nurse sharks breathe when they seem to be sleeping? Nurse sharks have strong muscles that let them push water from their cheeks over their gills while they rest. This helps them absorb oxygen from the water, so they don't need to swim all the time in order to breathe.

**MATES AND ROOMMATES**   Nurse sharks are social. They will share resting spaces with other nurse sharks. Sometimes, a cove or reef becomes so crowded with nurse sharks that they rest on top of one another.

# Wobbegongs

The wobbegong is a messy-looking shark that some people think resembles an unmade bed. Wobbegongs have enlarged barbels—whiskerlike growths—on their nostrils that cover their jaws and mouths. There are many different types of barbels, including some that look like lace. Epaulette sharks are closely related to wobbegongs.

There are 12 wobbegong species that range from 4 to 6 feet long and weigh up to 75 pounds. They live on sandy ledges or the floor of the ocean in areas from Japan to Australia and eat bottom-dwelling creatures like crustaceans and octopuses.

*Tasselled wobbegong*

*Banded wobbegong*

*Spotted wobbegong*

## AMBUSHERS

Wobbegongs are experts at camouflage and sneak attacks. They can sit on the ocean floor without moving for days. They are not good swimmers and don't chase their prey; instead, they reach out and grab it when it is nearby.

*Cobbler wobbegong*

Under a wobbegong's shaggy or lacey barbels, it has strong jaws and pointy teeth that look like fangs, with two rows on the top and three on the bottom.

*Spotted wobbegong*

## BITS & BITES

Wobbegongs are tenacious, which means that once they bite something they don't let go. Divers who accidentally step on wobbegongs find that they get severe bites and deep lacerations.

# Whale Sharks

At more than 40 feet long, whale sharks are the largest fish in the ocean, and at maturity they weigh about 70,000 pounds. It is their size that earned them their name—they are bigger than some whales, which are classified as mammals rather than fish and are the largest creatures of all. These huge sharks feed on small bites—plankton, the tiny organisms that drift through the ocean, and small, soft fish.

There's another difference between the big whale sharks and other, smaller carpetsharks: Whale sharks roam the open ocean, while most other carpetsharks stay on the ocean floor in specific areas.

## TIDBIT

**Gentle Giants**
Whale sharks are not aggressive. They ignore or swim away from humans when they see them.

## SPOTS AND STRIPES

Whale shark skin has a unique pattern, with vertical stripes from the head to the tail and spots all over. Like some others, whale sharks have toothy projections called dermal denticles, or skin teeth, all over their bodies.

## PARTY TIME!

Whale sharks are solitary creatures most of the time, but they sometimes gather in large groups to feast on plentiful food. In what is considered the world's largest gathering of whale sharks to date, more than 400 of them were seen together near Mexico's Yucatan Peninsula in the spring of 2011. Studies have shown that whale sharks travel to areas where fish are being born in large numbers, so no matter how many of the sharks show up there is enough food for all of them.

## FIN FACT

**Big Mouths** Whale sharks have very large mouths, sometimes up to 15 feet wide. They don't eat big things, but they gulp huge amounts of water full of plankton and small fish.

# The Nose Knows

Can sharks smell? Yes! Large volumes of water pass over the shark's rostrum (its snout) as it swims through the water. As it does so, water passes through their nostrils and over their smell sensors. These are highly developed and give sharks a great sense of smell. A shark can smell a tiny bit of fish blood or guts—even though it is dissolved in water—once it hits the shark's smell sensors.

**Following a scent:** Once a shark recognizes the scent of prey or food, it will turn and follow the scent until it gets to the prey. As the shark gets closer, the scent gets stronger and the shark knows it is going in the right direction.

## FACT OR FICTION?

Many people think sharks can smell tiny amounts of blood in the ocean, but is this fact or fiction? A team of Discovery Shark Week experts decided to find out. They put some lemon sharks in a big fish tank and then added a small amount of blood to the water and observed the sharks' behavior. The sharks reacted and followed the blood—but not until it had traveled through the water and reached their nostrils. The conclusion: Sharks can recognize just a few molecules of blood—a tiny amount—and turn and follow the trail. But they don't smell anything until some of it reaches their nostrils.

### FAST FACT

How do sharks know which direction to turn when they smell something yummy in the water? If the scent is picked up by the right nostril, they turn right, and if it's picked up by the left nostril, they turn left.

Sharks have the same five senses people have—smell, vision, hearing, taste, and touch. They also have some amazing extra senses, including the ability to detect vibrations and changes in water pressure, and electroreception, which is an ability to detect electrical impulses that all living creatures emit. Some of a shark's senses are powerful on their own—when used together, they give sharks extraordinary abilities for hunting and survival.

# ORDER OF SENSES

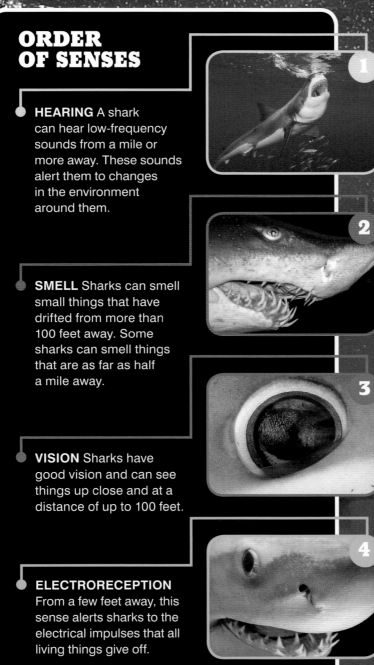

**HEARING** A shark can hear low-frequency sounds from a mile or more away. These sounds alert them to changes in the environment around them.

**SMELL** Sharks can smell small things that have drifted from more than 100 feet away. Some sharks can smell things that are as far as half a mile away.

**VISION** Sharks have good vision and can see things up close and at a distance of up to 100 feet.

**ELECTRORECEPTION** From a few feet away, this sense alerts sharks to the electrical impulses that all living things give off.

**TASTE AND TOUCH** From up close, sharks use taste and touch to sample foods and see if they are worth eating.

# Eyes on the Prey

Many people think sharks have poor eyesight, but scientists have determined that in most sharks their eyesight is actually quite good. Their eyes are similar to humans', with irises and pupils that control the amount of light that is let in and lenses that help them focus.

Sharks don't see their prey until it is about 100 feet from them. By that time, they are already aware of its presence because they have smelled its scent and felt its vibrations. At close range, vision takes over.

## LIGHT EYES, DARK EYES

Shark eyes are well adapted to their environment. Deep-sea sharks tend to have large, light-colored eyes that let in enough light for them to see in the murky depths. Sharks that swim nearer the surface have eyes that are darker and smaller to protect them from the bright light.

## NICTITATING MEMBRANE

Many species of sharks have a thin layer of skin called a nictitating membrane that is lowered over their eyes for protection from light or from injury during attack. Sharks that don't have nictitating membranes, including the great white, can roll their eyes back in the socket to protect them.

## TIDBIT

Most sharks have eyes on opposite sides of their heads. This allows them to see a wide stretch of what is around them. But they also have blind spots, places where they can't see at all, including the spot right in front of their noses.

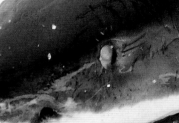

## MIRROR, MIRROR

How do sharks see in dark or murky waters? Most sharks have a mirrorlike reflector at the back of their eyes called a *tapetum lucidem*. This magnifies light and lets sharks see better in low light and focus on what's in front of them. Other animals—including cats, dogs, and raccoons—have the same mirrorlike reflectors in their eyes.

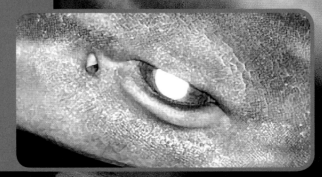

Sharks don't have ears on the outside of their bodies, but they do hear through an internal sound system. There is a tiny hole on each side of the top of a shark's head that leads to ducts filled with fluids that carry sound waves. These holes are called endolymphatic pores.

Sharks don't talk, of course, but scientists believe that sharks may be able to communicate with each other by emitting and hearing very low-frequency sounds. And sharks hear things like changes in water currents, which helps them stay balanced in the water and adjust their positions. Their hearing system makes them very good at picking up the low-frequency sounds that travel through the ocean waters. One of the sounds sharks hear is called the Yummy Hum. Too low for humans to hear, the Yummy Hum is a sound that dying fish emit and it lets sharks know there's something good to eat in the area.

Shark ears are inside their heads. The only visible part is a small hole on each side of the head, located where indicated above.

## BITS & BITES

Do sharks speak? They don't have vocal cords—which are essential to human speech—and there hasn't been evidence of sharks making vocal sounds. There are some sand sharks that bark like dogs, but scientists believe they are probably just expelling air.

## TOUCH

A shark's sense of touch isn't highly developed, and it doesn't rely on this sense as much as it does on other senses. When sharks want to identify an object to see if it's edible, they may bump it with their mouths and noses. But they have sensors all over their bodies that can feel changes in water pressure and water temperature. This alerts them to danger from predators and it lets them know when to migrate to cooler or warmer waters.

## TASTE

Sharks have taste buds in their mouths, but not on their tongues (which is where human taste buds are located). Sharks sometimes use their sense of taste to identify food to eat, tasting something to see if it has the fat and protein content they need. When a shark doesn't like the way something tastes, it spits it out.

Sharks have several senses that people and most other animals don't have. These help them survive in the deep waters of the sea, hunt for and catch their prey, and live very long lives.

**Electroreception** Sharks have a special sense, called electroreception, and it is this sense that makes them super predators. Electroreception—the ability to receive electrical impulses—lets them detect electrical waves that all living creatures give off, and makes them aware of every living thing in their path. Sharks sense electrical impulses through a network of pores on their heads and snouts leading to jelly-filled canals. These are called ampullae of Lorenzini and they can pick up a weak electrical impulse and send a signal to the shark's brain. This means sharks can unearth prey that is hiding motionless under sand.

### GUESS WHAT?

Active sharks have up to 1,500 ampullae of Lorenzini, while less active ones have only a few hundred.

## LATERAL LINES

A shark's sense of touch is not particularly sharp, but they have another sense that makes up for it. Sharks have lateral lines—a series of tubes that are spaced along a shark's body. These tubes contain sensory organs similar to the nerve endings in human skin. When water pours over the tubes and hits these lateral lines, the shark's brain senses vibrations and is alerted to nearby activity—such as prey or predators swimming, creating motion in the water.

## PIT ORGANS

Sharks have a series of pockets under their skin that contain sensory hair cells; these are called pit organs. No one has yet figured out exactly how these work, but they may help a shark feel water currents and other activity around it.

**FRILLED SHARKS**
*Chlamydoselachidae*

Frilled Shark
South African Frilled Shark

**COWSHARKS**
*Hexanchidae*

Bigeye Sixgill Shark
Bluntnose Sixgill Shark
Broadnose Sevengill Shark
Sharpnose Sevengill Shark

*Sevengill shark*

# Frilled Sharks and Cowsharks

## Highlights

### ORDER

Frilled sharks and Cowsharks *Hexanchiformes*

### NAME

Frilled sharks are named for a frilly patch over their gills. The origin of the name "cowshark" is not known, but it may be due to the cowshark's heavy body and slow movement.

### SPECIES

There are two frilled sharks and four cowsharks.

### SIZE

Frilled sharks are around 5 feet long; cowsharks range from 5 to 14 feet long.

### HABITAT

Frilled sharks and cowsharks live in cool, deep waters in scattered locations in coastal Atlantic and Pacific waters, with some off the southern coast of Africa.

Sharks in the same order don't necessarily look alike, and that's true of the frilled sharks and six- and sevengill sharks called cowsharks. Frilled sharks look more like eels or snakes than sharks. But all these sharks have some things in common, including extra gills, big mouths, eyes on the sides of their heads, spineless back fins, and an arrangement of vertebrae that's different from most other sharks. Both groups live in the deep sea.

Frilled sharks and cowsharks don't have many of the modern features of other sharks, including better senses, a more efficient digestive system, and jaws that are not connected to their heads (which would let them thrust their heads forward to catch prey). Called fossil sharks, frilled sharks and cowsharks have skeletons that resemble fossils of the earliest sharks; many scientists believe that they are closely related to sharks that lived more than 300 million years ago.

Frilled sharks have frilly coverings on their gills.

With their long, snakelike bodies, frilled sharks look like eels. Their mouths are especially big and are filled with sharp teeth; frilled sharks look like mouths with tails. They fit their long, narrow bodies into tight spaces from which they can ambush their prey.

Frilled sharks have 300 razor-sharp teeth in 25 rows.

# FAMILY MATTERS

Scientists at the Seattle Aquarium are studying a group of bluntnose sixgill sharks that appeared in nearby Puget Sound. The scientists attached tracking devices to the sharks and created a feeding station where the sharks could be observed. They found that pups born in the same litter stuck together for many months, with brothers and sisters swimming and feeding in pairs and groups. The scientists plan to keep following them and to look for other species that have the same habits.

Bluntnose sixgill sharks usually stay deep—down to 6,000 feet—where they are hard to study, but they come up to shallower waters to feed. They can catch prey easily, with sudden bursts of lightning speed and sharp teeth on the sides of their mouths.

# The Evolution of Sharks

Some sharks were born with features that made them better able to survive. A shark with a useful feature would pass along that feature to its offspring. Over millions of years, this happened from generation to generation. Sharks with superior features reproduced rapidly and sharks without those features died off because they couldn't compete successfully for food and mates. One example of this can be found in the special way shark jaws work. Scientists believe that the first sharks with jaws that were not fused to their heads appeared about 200 million years ago. This gave them the ability to thrust their jaws forward and catch prey efficiently. Today, many sharks have this feature.

## 400 MILLION YEARS AGO

Antarctilamne, found in Antarctica, was an eel-like fish. It is classified among the prehistoric sharks known as xenacanths. Antarctica is the only place where living sharks have not been found.

## 370 MILLION YEARS AGO

One of the earliest sharks, cladoselache, had cartilage, fins, and gills. It was 3 feet long and swam well, but its jaw was fused to its head so it couldn't thrust its head forward like today's sharks. It had smooth skin that wasn't as well protected from injury as that of later sharks.

## 280 MILLION YEARS AGO

Catastrophes such as earthquakes, floods, and freezes killed many of the earliest fish and insects. But many sharks survived, including stethacanthus, a fast-swimming shark with a very odd flat-topped, brushy fin. It also had toothlike scales on its skin, called dermal denticles, which prevented injury. During this era, sharks developed their unique feature of quickly replacing teeth that fall from their jaws.

## 180 MILLION YEARS AGO

A group of sharks called hybodonts arose. They were similar to today's bullheads, and, like bullheads, they had different kinds of teeth—sharp ones at the front of their mouths for biting and flatter ones at the sides for grinding. This group became extinct at the same time that dinosaurs vanished from the earth.

## 120 MILLION YEARS AGO

An increase in the population of small fish in the oceans made feeding easier for sharks and there was a big growth in new types of sharks. Sharks in this era developed jaws that were not fused to their skull and could thrust forward, making them efficient hunters. Their fins became more flexible, allowing for smoother swimming, and their teeth were replaced at a more rapid rate. Most sharks living today are similar to the sharks of this period.

Sharks first appeared about 400 million years ago. Since then, they have undergone many changes to evolve into the sharks of today.

## HOW DO SHARK EXPERTS KNOW?

Scientists study fossilized bones to learn how creatures evolved. But sharks don't have bones; they have cartilage, which dissolves quickly in ocean water. Luckily, after some sharks died, their bodies lay on rocks, leaving a fossilized impression on the rocks. Studying these gives good clues about shark evolution.

Some of the most startling shark fossils that have been found belong to megalodon, a species of shark that survived for more than 50 million years and became extinct about 35 million years ago. All that is left of it are teeth and jaws and, based on the size of these, scientists think that megalodon was more than 50 feet long—about three times the size of an average great white shark. Because it was so big, scientists assume that megalodon was the most terrifying predator in the seas, and it may have been fiercer than the great white. But it did not have the same ability to evolve and survive. Great white sharks came before it, and are still around today.

**WORD!**
Megalodon means "big tooth."

## BITS & BITES

There are shark teeth and impressions all over the world, some in places far from the ocean. That's because most of the earth, including all of North America, was covered by water millions of years ago, so prehistoric sharks swam all over it.

Scientists have found fossil evidence of at least 2,000 different species that have become extinct over the past 400 million years. One of the most unusual is helicoprion. Fossils of helicoprion show a tooth that looks like a cross between a circular saw and a pizza cutter. Scientists are studying the fossils to learn more about this impressive feature.

Opposite page: A model of megalodon's jaw.

Right: An artist's recreation of megalodon.

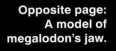

### BRAMBLE SHARKS
*Echinorhinidae*

Bramble Shark
Prickly Shark

### DOGFISH SHARKS
*Squalidae*

Fatspine Spurdog
Japanese Spurdog
Longnose Spurdog
Mandarin Dogfish
Roughskin Spurdog
Shortnose Spurdog
Shortspine Spurdog
Spiny or Piked Dogfish
Western Highfin Spurdog
Western Longnose Spurdog

### GULPER SHARKS
*Centrophoridae*

Arrowhead Dogfish
Birdbeak Dogfish
Blackfin Gulper Shark
Dumb Gulper Shark
Dwarf Gulper Shark
Gulper Shark
Leafscale Gulper Shark
Little Gulper Shark
Longnose Dogfish
Longnose Gulper Shark
Longsnout Dogfish
Lowfin Gulper Shark
Mosaic Gulper Shark
Needle Dogfish
Rough Longnose Dogfish
Smallfin Gulper Shark
Taiwan Gulper Shark
Western Gulper Shark

### LANTERN SHARKS
*Etmopteridae*

African Lanternshark
Bareskin Dogfish
Black Dogfish
Blackbelly Lanternshark
Blackmouth Lanternshark
Blurred Smooth Lanternshark
Broadband Dogfish
Brown Lanternshark
Caribbean Lanternshark
Combtooth Dogfish
Combtooth Lanternshark
Cylindrical Lanternshark
Densescale Lanternshark
Dwarf Lanternshark
False Lanternshark
Fringefin Lanternshark
Giant Lanternshark
Granular Dogfish
Great Lanternshark
Green Lanternshark
Hawaiian Lanternshark
Highfin Dogfish
Hooktooth Dogfish
Lined Lanternshark
New Zealand Lanternshark
Ornate Dogfish
Pink Lanternshark
Pygmy Lanternshark
Rasptooth Dogfish
Shortfin Smooth Lanternshark
Shorttail Lanternshark
Slendertail Lanternshark
Smalleye Lanternshark
Smooth Lanternshark
Southern Lanternshark
Splendid Lanternshark

Tailspot Lanternshark
Taiwan Lanternshark
Tasmanian Lanternshark
Thorny Lanternshark
Velvet Belly
Viper Dogfish
West Indian Lanternshark
Whitefin Dogfish

### SLEEPER SHARKS
*Somniosidae*

Azores Dogfish
Frog Shark
Greenland Shark
Japanese Sleeper Shark
Japanese Velvet Dogfish
Knifetooth Dogfish
Largespine Velvet Shark
Little Sleeper Shark
Longnose Velvet Dogfish
Pacific Sleeper Shark
Plunket's Shark
Portuguese Dogfish
Roughskin Shark
Sherwood Dogfish
Shortnose Velvet Dogfish
Smallmouth Velvet Dogfish
Southern Sleeper Shark
Sparsetooth Dogfish
Velvet Dogfish
Whitetail Dogfish

### ROUGHSHARKS
*Oxynotidae*

Angular Roughshark
Caribbean Roughshark
Japanese Roughshark
Prickly Dogfish
Sailfin Roughshark

### KITEFIN SHARKS
*Dalatiidae*

Bartail Spurdog
Blacktailed Spurdog
Cookiecutter Shark
Cuban Dogfish
Cyrano Spurdog
Eastern Longnose Spurdog
Japanese Spurdog
Kitefin Shark
Largetooth
Cookiecutter Shark
Longnose Pygmy Shark
Pocket Shark
Pygmy Shark
Shortnose Spurdog
Shortspine Spurdog
Smalleye Pygmy Shark
South China
Cookiecutter Shark
Spined Pygmy Shark
Spotted Spiny Spurdog
Taillight Shark
Taiwanese Dogfish
Western Longnose Spurdog

# Bramble, Roughsharks, Lantern Sharks, and Other Dogfish Sharks

## Highlights

**ORDER**

Dogfish sharks
*Squaliformes*

**NAME**

Dogfish sharks earn their name—they tend to travel and hunt in packs, the way dogs do.

**SPECIES**

There are 120 species in the Dogfish Order.

**SIZE**

Smallest is the dwarf lanternshark, which averages 8 inches long and weighs less than 1 pound. Largest is the Greenland shark, which grows up to 21 feet long and weighs up to 2,200 pounds.

**HABITAT**

Worldwide

Dogfish sharks hold many records: the oldest, the smallest, the longest pregnancies, and the shark that has the biggest estimated population in the world. They have many physical things in common. For example, they all have two dorsal fins, five sets of gills, and mouths underneath their snouts. They also have differences: The dogfish group includes a slow, stout 20-footer, some sharks that glow in the dark, and the aptly named cookiecutter shark that takes cookie-shaped bites from prey. There are dogfish sharks all over the world, from warm tropical seas to cold arctic waters, shallow and deep, and many of them hunt in large groups.

# Spiny Dogfish

Spiny dogfish are on the small side for sharks—they average around 3 feet long—but there are a lot of them. Spiny dogfish are considered to be the most abundant shark in the world. They are common fish for people to eat and in the past 20 years their numbers have decreased by about 95 percent and they are now considered endangered. There are quotas in many states and countries for how many of these sharks can be harvested each year, to ensure they aren't overfished.

Many dogfish species, including whitespotted spurdogs shown below, form large packs to chase after prey. These packs often consist of like types—all males, all females, all young, all older.

## BITS & BITES

Spiny dogfish have spines on the base of their dorsal fins. When they are attacked, they curl up or arch their backs to point the spines at the attacker.

Spiny dogfish are not popular with commercial fishing boats. They will bite through fishing nets to get at halibut or mackerel being caught and hauled in, and then the fishing boat loses the catch. Spiny dogfish—like this one—are often caught up in fishing nets as "bycatch"— fish taken up in nets that are intended for other species. This contributes to their declining population.

## LEGEND AND LORE

The dogfish shark appears in the legends and lore of the native peoples of the northwest Pacific coast called the Haida. The Dogfish Woman is the legend of a woman who transformed herself into a dogfish to visit the undersea world. One of their most revered icons, Dogfish Woman is a symbol of power, leadership, and the ability to overcome seemingly insurmountable obstacles.

# Greenlands and Lanterns

*Velvet belly shark*

## BUILT-IN FLASHLIGHTS

Most lantern sharks carry their own light source wherever they go. Like glowworms and fireflies, they have useful organs called photophores (FOE-toe-fourz) that glow when needed. Lantern sharks live in deep, dark waters, so their own little lights are very helpful when they need to see their prey or when they want to be visible for mating.

### LIVING LIGHT

The process by which lantern sharks glow is called bioluminescence, a long word that means "living light." Here are some other bright creatures.

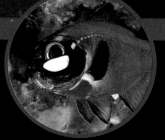

**Flashlight fish**
have organs under their eyes that contain luminous bacteria.

**Jellyfish**
can detach glowing tentacles and leave them behind to fool predators.

# FROM TINY TO TREMENDOUS

Members of the Dogfish Order range in size from the smallest shark of all, the dwarf lanternshark, to one of the largest sharks in the world, the Greenland shark.

Dwarf lanternshark (above), the smallest shark of all, Greenland shark (right), number six on the list of largest sharks.

## GREENLAND SHARKS

Greenland sharks are long, large, and slow. This deep-sea shark can survive in freezing waters, and it is the northernmost of all sharks. Greenland sharks generally swim about a mile below the ocean's surface.

Their small eyes attract parasites, which can make it hard for them to see. There is a bonus, however. The parasites are bioluminescent, and their glow attracts prey for the Greenland sharks to eat.

**Lanternfish**
emit yellow, blue, or green light depending on the species.

**Squid**
that live in the deep sea have photophores all over their bodies.

**Firefly**
There are bioluminescent creatures on land, too.

# What's on the Menu?

Different sharks eat different foods, but all sharks are carnivores, which means that they eat meat. Sharks eat a diverse range of animals found in the ocean. In general, bigger sharks look for bigger prey, but the two largest sharks eat some of the smallest creatures in the ocean.

**DON'T CHEW YOUR FOOD!**

The upper and lower parts of a shark's jaw are hinged in a way that makes it difficult for the lower part to move separately from the upper part, so they don't chew their food the way people do. Sharks catch and hold prey in their strong jaws and use their sharp teeth to tear it into pieces small enough to swallow. Some sharks, such as nurse sharks, can use their mouth like a vacuum cleaner, to suck food right in.

**Zooplankton**, also called **plankton**, is the name for a variety of small organisms that drift through bodies of water, including insects, jellyfish, and baby fish. Whale and basking (shown below) sharks eat zooplankton.

**Cephalopods**, such as squid, octopus, and cuttlefish, have big heads and lots of tentacles. Many small sharks, including blue sharks (shown below) and angelsharks, feast on cephalopods.

**Mollusks** and **crustaceans** such as lobsters, crabs, clams, and shrimp, are hard-shelled creatures. Sharks that eat them, like bullhead sharks (shown below), have special teeth that can crush through the hard shells.

Food gives sharks the energy they need to swim around all day and night. Luckily, sharks are experts at all the jobs they must do to nourish themselves: choosing the right food for their bodies, finding, catching, and eating it. And they have awesome jaws, teeth, and digestive systems to help them.

**Larger fish** like tuna and bluefish are eaten by bigger sharks, including makos. Bigger sharks, including the mako shown below, also eat smaller sharks.

**Marine mammals**, **sea turtles**, and **seabirds**—animals other than fish that live near and swim in the ocean—are prey for larger sharks like tiger sharks and the great white shown below.

**Skates** and **rays**—flat, diamond-shaped fish—are also food for sharks, including hammerhead sharks.

# Favorite Foods

Many sharks seem to have a favorite food, usually something they are especially good at catching or that gives them a high dose of nourishment.

## ANDY SAYS

Though many people think that sharks will eat anything, they are actually selective eaters. All you have to do is look at shark teeth to know that each species has a unique diet. For example, great white sharks have pointed, serrated teeth for tearing through blubbery seals; sand tiger sharks have smooth, pointy teeth for puncturing and trapping fish; horn sharks have flat, platelike teeth for crushing mussel shells; and tiger sharks have teeth that are serrated and curved back for tearing through turtle shells. In an aquarium setting, sharks can be very picky and often refuse to eat a food item they have eaten for months because they want something else.

—*Andy Dehart, Marine Biologist*

**Thresher sharks eat small fish. They can use their long tails to whip them into position to be eaten.**

**Bronze whaler sharks eat small, bony fish like sardines. Once a year, millions of sardines migrate up the coast of eastern Africa. No one is sure why the sardines do it, but bronze whalers and other sharks are there to feed on them.**

**WORD!**
Prey is any creature that is hunted by another animal as food.

Great whites hunt and eat seals and sea lions. These blubbery animals are full of the fat and protein that big sharks need.

# Open Wide: Teeth

Sharks come in different sizes and shapes, and with different attitudes—but they all have teeth. Sharks' teeth and strong jaws are adapted to the way sharks live, hunt, and eat. Huge basking and whale sharks eat soft foods such as plankton and small fish; they have tiny teeth called gill rakers that filter all the seawater that comes into their mouths, separating the food (which is then swallowed) from other stuff. Bulls, blue sharks, and wobbegongs have sharp, curvy teeth that are good for trapping fast-moving prey. Tiger sharks and great whites have big, pointy teeth to bite down on their prey and tear the flesh apart.

## FAST FACT

A shark can grow and chomp through up to 50,000 teeth in its lifetime.

Like most sharks, this shortfin mako shark's teeth grow in rows.

## BITE ME

Cookiecutters are small sharks (1 to 2 feet long) with unique eating habits. They clamp on to their prey, then pivot to take out a cookie-shaped piece of flesh. There are fish all over the sea that escaped this toothy predator and have cookie-shaped scars on their bodies, like the spinner dolphin at right.

## CHOMPER ROWS

Sharks can have anywhere from two to as many as 300 rows of teeth, depending on the species. The teeth don't have roots, so they fall out easily. But sharks have a unique tooth replacement system. When a tooth falls out, another one moves up from the row behind to take its place in as little as a day or two.

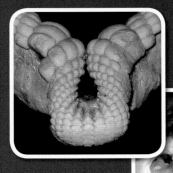

A horn shark's flat teeth crush its food.

A sand tiger's sharp teeth pierce fast-swimming fish.

1 Huge tooth of the more than 50-foot megalodon, which lived millions of years ago.

2 Great white shark teeth have sawlike serrations, which makes them very good at cutting.

3 Makos use their pointy teeth to pierce and trap fast-moving prey.

4 Tiger sharks have curvy, pointy teeth that are sharp enough to puncture metal.

## JAWS OF DEATH

Many sharks can thrust their jaws out to catch their prey, because the jaws are not firmly attached to the skull. A shark will push its jaws forward and bite down with the upper jaw. Then, when the prey is in place, the shark will tear it apart with its lower teeth. If the food item is not already inside the shark's mouth after it is bitten, then the shark will tear it into smaller pieces by shaking its head back and forth. The upper teeth are pulled back to hold the food in place while the lower teeth do the cutting while the shark shakes the food violently to rip it apart.

# Hunting Habits

Sharks have sharp teeth, strong jaws, extraordinary senses, and many other advantages when it comes to hunting for food. One disadvantage is that their food keeps trying to swim away. Luckily for them, sharks have techniques and tricks that help them outwit their prey.

## FEEDING FRENZY

A feeding frenzy can occur when a shark sees that another shark has found something good to eat and joins in. As more and more sharks join the group and fight over the food, the feeding frenzy can get intense and bloody. Feeding frenzies with hundreds of sharks fighting over the same bits of flesh have been observed, and sometimes the sharks end up biting one another.

*Mako shark*

*Tasselled wobbegong*

*Tiger shark*

*Bull shark*

## SPEED

Sharks are fast. Some swim up to 30 miles per hour or faster and can outswim most of the fastest fish. The shortfin mako, clocked at a speed of 44 miles per hour, is one of the few fish that can swim fast enough to catch a bluefin tuna.

## AMBUSH

Sharks like this wobbegong can camouflage themselves on the ocean bottom and stay very still for hours or days. When a smaller fish or shellfish comes near, they pounce.

## DECEPTION

Tiger sharks have been observed swimming quietly past prey, allowing the other fish to feel safe. Then they turn back and attack the unsuspecting fish.

## CHARGE!

Bull sharks are not subtle at all. They head-butt their prey to see if it's something good to eat. This maneuver is called "bump and bite."

## FINBACK CATSHARKS
### Proscylliidae
African Ribbontail Catshark
Clown or Magnificent Catshark
Cuban Ribbontail Catshark
Graceful Catshark
Harlequin Catshark
Pygmy Ribbontail Catshark

## FALSE CATSHARKS
### Pseudotriakidae
False Catshark
Flatnose Catshark
Pygmy False Catshark
Slender Smoothhound
  or Gollumshark
Sulu Gollumshark
Whitemouthed Gollumshark

## CATSHARKS
### Scyliorhinidae
African Sawtail Catshark
African Spotted Catshark
Antilles Catshark
Arabian Catshark
Atlantic Ghost Catshark
Atlantic Sawtail Catshark
Australian Marbled Catshark
Australian Reticulate
  Swellshark
Australian Sawtail Catshark
Australian Spotted Catshark
Australian Swellshark
Bali Catshark
Balloon Shark
Banded Sand Catshark
Beige Catshark
Bighead Catshark
Black Roughscale Catshark
Blackfin Sawtail
Blackgill Catshark
Blackmouth Catshark
Blackspotted Catshark
Blacktip Sawtail Catshark
Blotched Catshark

Blotchy Swellshark
Boa Catshark
Bristly Catshark
Broadbelly Catshark
Broadfin Sawtail Catshark
Broadgill Catshark
Broadhead Catshark
Broadmouth Catshark
Broadnose Catshark
Brown Catshark or Plain Happy
Brown Shyshark
Brownspotted Catshark
Campeche Shark
Chain Catshark
Circle-blotch Pygmy Swellshark
Cloudy Catshark
Comoro Catshark
Cook's Swellshark
Coral Catshark
Dark Shyshark or Pretty Happy
Deepwater Catshark
Draughtsboard Shark
Dusky Catshark
Dwarf Catshark
Dwarf Sawtail Catshark
Eastern, Natal Shyshark,
  or Happy Chappie
Fat Catshark
Federov's Catshark
Filetail Catshark
Flaccid Catshark
Flagtail Swellshark
Flathead Catshark
Freckled Catshark
Galapagos Catshark
Gecko Catshark
Ghost Catshark
Grinning Izak
Gulf Catshark
Hoary Catshark
Honeycomb Izak
Humpback Catshark
Iceland Catshark

Indian Swellshark
Izak Catshark
Izu Catshark
Japanese Catshark
Largenose Catshark
Leopard Catshark
Leopard-spotted Swellshark
Lined Catshark
Lizard Catshark
Lollipop Catshark
Longfin Catshark
Longfin Sawtail Catshark
Longnose Catshark
Longnose Sawtail Catshark
McMillan's Catshark
Mouse Catshark
Mud Catshark
Narrowbar Swellshark
Narrowtail Catshark
New Caledonia Catshark
New Zealand Catshark
New Zealand Filetail
Northern Draughtsboard
  Swellshark
Northern Sawtail Catshark
Nursehound
Onefin Catshark
Orange Spotted Catshark
Painted Swellshark
Pajama Shark
  or Striped Catshark
Pale Catshark
Pale Spotted Catshark
Panama Ghost Catshark
Peppered Catshark
Pinocchio Catshark
Polkadot Catshark
Puffadder Shyshark
  or Happy Eddie
Quagga Catshark
Red East African Spotted
  Catshark or Grinning Izak
Redspotted Catshark
Reticulated Swellshark

Roughskin Catshark
Roughtail Catshark
Saddled Swellshark
Salamander Shark
Saldanha Catshark
Sarawak Pygmy Swellshark
Shortnose Demon Catshark
Shorttail Catshark
Slender Catshark
Slender Sawtail Catshark
Smallbelly Catshark
Smalldorsal Catshark
Smalleye Catshark
Smallfin Catshark
Small-spotted Catshark
Smoothbelly Catshark
Sombre Catshark
South China Catshark
Southern Sawtail Catshark
Spatulasnout Catshark
Speckled Catshark
Speckled Swellshark
Spongehead Catshark
Spotless Catshark
Spotted Swellshark
Springer's Sawtail Catshark
Steven's Swellshark
Stout Catshark
Swell Shark
Tiger Catshark
Tropical Izak
Variegated Catshark
Velvet Catshark
West African Catshark
Western Spotted Catshark
White Ghost Catshark
White-bodied Catshark
White-clasper Catshark
Whitefin Swellshark
Whitesaddled Catshark
White-tip Catshark
Yellowspotted Catshark

# Catsharks

There are 160 catshark species and more are discovered and named every year. Catsharks have almond-shaped eyes, sometimes green or gold, and slender bodies. They have adapted to their environment in many ways. Many catsharks have patterned skin—stripes, dots, and some attractive and unusual markings—that help camouflage them. Like other groundsharks, catsharks have two dorsal fins, an anal fin, a protective nictitating membrane over their eyes and five gill slits.

## Highlights

### ORDER
Catsharks
*Carcharhiniformes*

### NAME
Catsharks have beautiful, catlike eyes.

### SPECIES
160 species in three families.

### SIZE
Most are about 2 feet long; some reach 5 feet long.

### HABITAT
Catsharks live in many habitats, from deep sea to coastline; tropical to arctic waters.

Catsharks are part of the Groundshark Order, the largest shark order, with more than 270 different species. Other members of the Groundshark Order are hammerheads, houndsharks, requiem sharks, and weasel sharks.

**M**any members of the Groundshark Order are beautiful, but none surpasses the spectacular chain catshark. Its creamy-yellow body is covered with a dark brown pattern that looks like a chain. Bright turquoise eyes complete the picture. Chain catsharks live on the east coast of North America, from New England down to the Gulf of Mexico. The deep waters off North Carolina and Virginia are particularly attractive to them. They live in rocky, ocean-floor environments, with plentiful crevices in which they can hide and where they are camouflaged by their patterned bodies.

## LOOKING GOOD

From their distinctive skin markings to their colorful eyes, catsharks display many interesting features.

Oval green eye of a small-spotted catshark

Black-and-white pattern on a coral catshark

Chain catsharks often stay motionless on the ocean floor for days.

## MERMAID'S PURSE

Catsharks, including chain catsharks, lay eggs in sacs called mermaid's purses. The purses have stringy tendrils, so they can be secured to a rock while the egg grows big enough to hatch. Catshark pups develop fully in these purses. By the time they are ready to hatch, they have outgrown the egg sac and break through to swim away. Catshark egg cases are under 4 inches long. Embryos curl up inside to fit.

Spots on a
blackspotted catshark

Tawny stripes
of a swell shark

Graceful body of a
gulf catshark

# Pajamas and Leopards

The pajama shark and the leopard catshark are closely related. They both live in the same small area off the coast of southern Africa. Both are small and typically measure 2 to 3 feet long, with the leopard on the smaller side. They have similar sharp, pointy teeth. They live on the ocean floor and on continental shelves and hunt the same type of food—including small, bony fish and octopuses. But pajama sharks and leopard catsharks look different in striking ways. The skin of each type of shark has unique patterns and colors—and it's easy to see how each of them got its name.

Filetail catsharks like the one above have a row of sharp denticles (toothlike projections) at the end of their tails. The sharp points make them hard to swallow. Filetail catsharks live in the waters off the west coast of the U.S.

## LEOPARD SPOTS

Leopard catsharks come in different patterns, although those that live in the same area tend to sport similar looks to one another. Leopard catshark colors range from pale yellow to jet black, and the spots can be round, blotchy, or rose shaped.

Unlike the leopard catshark's patterns, which vary from shark to shark, the pajama shark's stripes always look alike. Each shark has seven stripes running from head to tail, with one in the middle and three on each side.

Catsharks are small and they have to defend themselves from predators that are much bigger than they are, including many other kinds of sharks. They have clever ways to do this.

Swell sharks can swell up out of water—they swallow air to double in size. When the swell shark expels the air, it makes a sound like a dog's bark.

Swell sharks have a nifty way of staying alive—they swell up. When they see a predator approaching, they grab their tail fins with their teeth so that their bodies are U-shaped and then start swallowing water until they balloon up to double their size, as in the photo above. This makes them look bigger and scarier so some predators, thinking they are too small to win a fight, turn away.

Happy Eddie is the nickname scientists have given the puffadder shyshark, a 2-foot-long catshark. It got the name "puffadder" because its orange spots and brown stripes resemble those of the puff adder viper, a venomous snake. Puffadder shysharks are usually the losers in fights with fur seals, which often throw them in the air before killing them. Happy Eddie has a solution: It curls itself into a tight ball and covers its eyes with its tail. Scientists assume that this makes it less easy to swallow, so predators leave it alone. Other catsharks, including pajama sharks and leopard catsharks, do this as well.

The puff adder viper, which the puffadder shyshark resembles.

## BITS & BITES

Shysharks are not aggressive and spend a lot of time resting in protected places. Sometimes, two or more shysharks rest together.

Happy Eddie did not get its name because it is particularly happy. Instead, "Happy" comes from its scientific name, *Haploblepharus edwardsii.* "Haploblepharus" means "single eyelash" and probably refers to the nictitating membrane, a protective membrane that covers the eyes of most catsharks. The "Eddie" part was given to honor George Edwards, an artist and naturalist who discovered this species in 1760.

# What a Cute Baby!

In most shark species, the pups grow inside the female shark until they are ready to be born. They are born underwater and can swim right away. Some sharks lay eggs in protected cases outside their bodies. There is usually one pup in each case, but a female shark can lay dozens or even hundreds of eggs. Some sharks carry eggs inside their body; the pups hatch inside the mother's body, then are born live.

Lemon sharks give birth to live young.

**1**

## BORN SWIMMING
In some shark species the pups grow inside a female shark until they've developed enough to live on their own. How long this takes, and how many pups develop in a single pregnancy, vary by shark species. Female sharks can be pregnant anywhere from three months to two years or more. The pups are born underwater and can swim right away.

**2**

## EGGS INSIDE
Whale sharks and tiger sharks are two of the species that carry eggs in sacs within the female shark's body. When they are ready to be born, pups first hatch from the egg sacs inside the female shark and then are born as live pups. Some species of sharks can carry up to 300 eggs within their bodies at any one time.

*Tiger shark*

Before a great white shark becomes a 3,000-pound predator, it starts out as a pup. That's the first stage in a shark's life, and for the first few years pups grow into their full size and learn how to hunt and protect themselves. It takes a long time before sharks can have babies of their own and are considered adults.

**3**

## EGGS OUTSIDE

Catsharks, horn sharks, and zebra sharks are some of the species that lay eggs in protective cases outside their bodies. There is usually one pup in each case, but a female shark may lay dozens or even hundreds of egg cases in a year. The cases are thick and leathery to provide protection. Pups emerge from the cases when they are ready to survive in the outside world.

*Horn shark*

# The First Years of Life

For any species to survive, it has to have babies and the babies have to live long enough to have babies of their own. Sharks don't raise their offspring the way people do, but they have ways of ensuring that pups survive and grow. Some species, particularly bullheads, lay their eggs in safe places and position them securely in crevices so that they don't crack or float away on the current. Others—bull and tiger sharks, for example—give birth in estuaries and coves, where they are protected from the dangers of the open ocean.

Shark pups are not defenseless when they are born. They are born or hatch fully nourished, and while they can swim right away, they don't need to hunt for food for the first few weeks of their lives. Shark pups are born with sharp teeth and the ability to use them—many scientists who do research with newborn pups have been bitten by the adorable little sharks.

## STAYING ALIVE

A shark pup's biggest problem is that it looks like a tasty tidbit for larger fish including other sharks. One strategy that young sharks use is to stay together and remain close to where they were born. There are protected bays and estuaries in many places—such as this one in the Bahamas—where females go to pup. The female sharks leave, but the pups stay in the bay for a few years before they set off on their own. Above, a lemon shark in a mangrove swamp that serves as a nursery.

## PUP FACTS

Female **bull sharks** are pregnant for about 11 months.

Female **horn sharks** carefully position their cone-shaped egg cases in safe places. The pups are born with enough nourishment to last them about a month, at which point they start eating on their own. Then they eat easy prey like small shrimp and worms.

**Bamboo sharks** are hatched from eggs in cases that settle on the ocean floor. The pups are 5 to 7 inches long when born.

### ANDY SAYS

Many of the places that provide refuge for baby sharks, like bays and estuaries, are also the areas most affected by human development. The Chesapeake and Delaware bays are perfect examples of this.

—Andy Dehart,
Marine Biologist

**Sixgill shark** litters of anywhere from 22 to 106 pups have been recorded. That's a lot of brothers and sisters!

# Ages and Stages

Different types of sharks start out at different sizes and grow at different rates, but they all go through key life stages as they grow.

**A FOUR-WEEK-OLD WHALE SHARK PUP**
When the pups are born, they're about 2 feet long. They have a lot of growing to do in the 30 years it takes them to reach adulthood and their full length of about 40 feet.

## SHARK TEENS

Although sharks start hunting soon after they are born, they don't have full biting power until they are adults. Scientists have used computer-generated 3-D models to show that great white sharks that are under 10 years old have weak bites because the cartilage that holds their jaws in place has not yet become as hard as it is in adults. When adolescent sharks try to bite big prey, they can't chew through it and usually spit it out. Smaller fish are easier for them to handle.

## REACHING MATURITY

Different shark species reach adulthood at different ages, and in many species the males and females reach maturity at different ages as well, but all sharks are considered adults when they are able to reproduce. This can be anywhere from two to three years for smoothhounds to 30 years for the whale shark. Sharks have a hard time surviving in the ocean, and getting to 30 years of age can be difficult. If they die before adulthood—because sharks are caught by people or eaten by other fish—they will not reproduce and help keep their species alive.

## MATING YEARS

For many shark species, including hammerheads and tigers, males find mates in a way that would be a bad idea for people: They bite the female—hard. Many female sharks have been found with scars from these bites. This is not unique to sharks, however. Turtles, tortoises, and cats also bite their potential mates. Female wobbegongs, great whites, and other species emit scented substances called pheromones (FAIR-oh-moans) to let males know that they are interested in mating.

*Adult whale shark*

## TIDBIT
Greenland sharks are among the slowest growers; some tagging experiments show that they grow only a quarter inch per year.

## DO SHARKS DIE OF OLD AGE?

The ocean is a brutal place, and anything that dies in it gets eaten by something else. If they are lucky enough to evade predators as they get older, sharks die from heart problems, liver problems, kidney failure, and other diseases—just like other animals.

## HOW LONG DO SHARKS LIVE?

It's hard to know the exact answer to this question, but scientists do know that sharks live long lives and that life spans vary by species. Here is what scientists have determined about some shark species and their life spans:

**Greenland sharks:** up to 200 years
**Spiny dogfish:** up to 100 years
**Whale sharks:** more than 100 years

**Hammerheads:** up to 30 years
**Porbeagle sharks:** about 26 years
**Blue sharks:** about 16 years

**9 SPECIES**

**HAMMERHEADS**
*Sphyrnidae*
Bonnethead
Great Hammerhead
Mallethead
Scalloped Hammerhead
Scoophead
Smalleye Hammerhead
Smooth Hammerhead
Whitefin Hammerhead
Winghead

*Scalloped hammerhead*

# Hammerhead Sharks

## Highlights

### ORDER

Groundsharks
*Carcharhiniformes*

### NAME

Hammerheads
are named for the
hammerlike shape
of their heads.

### SPECIES

There are nine species in
the hammerhead group.

### SIZE

The great hammerhead
is the largest in the
group. It averages
13 feet long but can
grow to 20 feet. Great
hammerheads can weigh
up to 1,000 pounds.
The bonnethead, the
smallest of the group,
is usually around
3 feet long and weighs
less than 7 pounds.

### HABITAT

Hammerheads live in
warm and tropical waters
all over the world.

Hammerheads are part
of the Groundshark
Order, the largest shark
order, with more than
270 different species.
Other members of the
Groundshark Order are
catsharks, houndsharks,
requiem sharks, and
weasel sharks.

**H**ammerheads are among the weirdest-looking creatures in the ocean. All hammerheads have long, narrow hammer-shaped heads called cephalofoils (seff-FAH-low-foils), with eyes at each end. When they swim through the ocean, hammerheads move their cephalofoils from side to side. Some scientists think that this motion helps them see better, keep their balance, or pick up electrical impulses from other creatures.

There are nine species in the hammerhead group, and each species has a slightly different cephalofoil, with different creases and bumps. The names of the species—such as bonnethead, scalloped, and smooth—describe these bumps and creases. Hammerheads are good hunters and use their heads when hunting down and killing their prey, which includes bony fish, squid, and stingrays.

# Smart Sharks

Hammerhead cephalofoils improve the shark's hunting skills in several ways. Hammerhead eyes are spaced far apart at each end of their heads, giving them nearly 360-degree vision, so they see prey in a much wider area of the ocean than other sharks. Their wide heads also have room for more ampullae of Lorenzini, the tiny sense organs that receive the electrical impulses that all living creatures give off. That makes them better able to locate other fish and ocean creatures. Many people think that hammerheads are smart because they are such good hunters.

**Eyes** The position of the eyes lets hammerheads see more of the edible creatures in their vicinity. It also gives them good depth perception, which means that they can sense how near or far away those creatures are.

*Scalloped hammerhead*

**Ampullae of Lorenzini** Hammerheads have extra helpings of these sensory organs and they are spread out over a wide surface, which makes the hammerhead especially good at finding prey. The ampullae make the heads like metal detectors, panning back and forth.

# SCALLOPED HAMMERHEAD

Scalloped hammerheads are the most common of all the hammerhead species. They swim in warm waters all over the world. Average females grow to about 8 feet long; males are smaller, usually under 6 feet.

Scientists believe that the population of scalloped hammerheads has decreased by up to 90 percent over the past 30 years. This species is particularly subject to overfishing because its fins are valuable for use in the delicacy shark fin soup.

## SPA DAY

Scalloped hammerheads are often covered by small parasites called copepods. The sharks occasionally visit "cleaning stations," areas where small fish clean the parasites off their skin.

*Smooth hammerhead*

## HAMMERPUPS

When baby hammerheads are born, their cephalofoils are curvy and also soft. That's good for the mother shark, because it would be hard to give birth to a pup with a wide, hard head. As the pups get older, the cephalofoils become straighter and firmer.

**M**any sharks are loners, but scalloped hammerheads tend to hang around in groups or schools. They join with hundreds of other scalloped hammerheads and swim around together for days. Each school of hammerheads forms a community, with some of the largest sharks in the center of the pack and younger ones on the outside. No one is sure why hammerheads form schools—many other sharks don't—but it may be to protect themselves from larger predators, to help them migrate to cooler waters in the summer, or to help males find mates.

At night, hammerheads leave their schools and hunt alone.

## DID YOU KNOW?

A group of hammerhead sharks is called a school, a shoal, or a shiver.

# DATING AND MATING

In a large school of scalloped hammerheads, the largest females are usually found in the middle of the pack. This makes them easier to find by the males that are ready to mate. Larger female hammerheads will usually give birth to the most pups—sometimes more than 50 of them.

After a male hammerhead chooses a female, he gives her a hard bite to let her know he's interested. The male and female then swim away from the school together.

Scientists who study hammerhead schools find that the sharks behave in some strange ways. They shake their heads when approaching other sharks and sometimes bump into them. They also sometimes "corkscrew" by twirling their bodies as they move downward. Some scientists think this behavior is part of courtship, while others think it is a form of aggression.

# Great Hammerheads

Great hammerheads are the biggest of the group. They are also one of the ten biggest sharks in the world. They are good predators, but they rarely attack people. Divers have reported that great hammerheads sometimes seem curious and swim around them, but when the divers try to approach, the big sharks swim away.

Hammerheads are very good at making turns in tight places. The arrangement of the hammerhead's vertebrae enables hammerheads to move their heads up and down easily and that's why they turn so well.

## DIFFERENCES

Hammerhead sharks have been around for millions of years, and different hammerhead species have developed different-shaped heads.

**The bonnethead,**
a small hammerhead species, has a cephalofoil that looks like an old-fashioned hat or bonnet.

**Scalloped hammerheads**
have ridges all along their cephalofoils. They're the third-largest hammerhead.

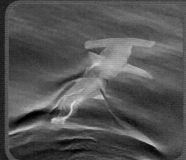

Hammerheads can dive to 1,600 feet but they sometimes swim just beneath the surface when migrating to cooler waters.

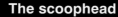

**The great hammerhead's** cephalofoil is the longest, straightest and most T-shaped of all the species

**The scoophead** is a small, rare species with a cephalofoil that is sometimes one-third the size of its entire body

Hammerheads have enormous mouths on the undersides of their huge T-shaped heads, but their mouths look small compared to the size of their heads. The position of their mouths makes them good at feeding on the ocean floor as well as in open water

# Shark Activities

Researchers observe sharks closely, looking for evidence that certain behaviors are intentional and not just accidental. They have found certain activities, such as fin flapping and browsing, happen regularly enough to indicate that they have some purpose. And scientists are also looking for evidence that some sharks, such as porbeagles, actually play with each other.

## BREACHING

Sharks swimming close to the surface sometimes leap right out of the water. This is called breaching and is usually done to catch prey on the surface. Great white sharks are famous for dramatic breaching when they are on the trail of seals; most of this activity takes place in South Africa—great whites in other places usually stay under the surface. Blacktips and thresher sharks sometimes leap out of the water as well. The showiest jumper is the spinner shark, which twirls around in the air, sometimes three or even four times, when breaching.

## BROWSING

Sharks skim over reefs, seeming to browse for things that might interest them. Underwater photographers say sharks often go after their camera equipment. This might be because they emit electrical impulses and the sharks think they are food. But many divers report that sharks seem genuinely curious.

## MIGRATING

Many sharks migrate, traveling great distances to find plentiful food or heading to warmer or cooler waters when seasons change. Some, such as the sandbar shark, migrate to find quiet places to give birth. Great white sharks have made incredible journeys, recorded by tracking devices. Blue sharks, like the one above, regularly travel from New York to Brazil, a distance of over 3,500 miles.

Sharks have two main activities: breathing and eating. In order to breathe, many sharks need to keep swimming so that water passes over their gills. In order to eat, they have to hunt and kill their prey. These activities keep them busy, but there are other things on their To Do list.

## FIN FLAPPING

Sharks sometimes slap the water with their fins or arch their backs. These may be ways they threaten or warn other sharks.

## SLEEPING

Do sharks sleep? Many of them need to keep swimming in order to keep water moving over their gills so that they can breathe. But some sharks, including the Caribbean reef shark shown above, look for places where the current is strong enough to flush water over their gills, and take short naps. Shark naps are more like rest periods, when they can shut down some functions, including brain activity. Dogfish sharks can rest while they are swimming because their swimming is controlled by their spines instead of by their brains. Other sharks can hold water in their cheeks and use their cheek muscles to push water over their gills while they sleep for up to 30 minutes at a time.

## DIVING

Sharks move to different depths for different reasons. Some sharks, including bull sharks like the one above, prefer warm water and will go into deeper or shallower waters in search of it. The spined pygmy shark, a small shark that measures less than a foot long, lives in deep water during the day and swims to the surface at night to find food in the upper levels of the ocean.

Sharks have a reputation for being loners, and most sharks live and hunt solo. But in many cases, sharks interact with other fish in surprising ways that benefit them both.

Lemon sharks like the ones below often spend time together. Sevengill sharks have been observed in groups of 18 or more, feeding at the same time without bothering one another. And occasionally different shark species hang out together—oceanic whitetip sharks are often seen with silky sharks.

## CLEANERS

Sharks are groomed by smaller fish, which eat parasites and debris stuck to their bodies. This keeps the sharks clean and healthy and provides a meal for the cleaners. The cleaners also get protection from other big fish that might eat them. Because it benefits both, this is called a symbiotic relationship.

Pilot fish are living toothbrushes. They swim into mouths of sharks and eat bits of food right off their teeth.

## FAST FACT

Sharks often visit areas where cleaner fish live when they need grooming, sometimes swimming long distances to get there.

## HITCHHIKERS

Remoras are fish that have suction cups on their heads. They use these suction cups to attach themselves to sharks' bodies. Remoras do not clean sharks, so only the remoras benefit from the relationship. The sharks sometimes seem bothered by the remoras, but allow them to hang on.

## DO SHARKS LIKE PEOPLE?

Sharks are not warm and cuddly, but they do seem to develop relationships with humans, just as other animals do in zoo and aquarium settings. Staff at aquariums and at shark feeding sites will often get to know individual sharks by working with them day after day and observe that the sharks may have different behaviors with the humans they interact with on a regular basis.

## ANDY SAYS

Many sharks are comfortable around humans, but I would not say they "like" human interaction. In fact, it is possible that a crowd of divers and snorkelers in the water may disrupt their feeding at certain locations.

—*Andy Dehart, Marine Biologist*

**BARBELED HOUNDSHARKS**
*Leptochariidae*
Barbeled Houndshark

**HOUNDSHARKS**
*Triakidae*
Arabian, Hardnose, or
Moses Smoothhound
Australian Grey Smoothhound
Banded Houndshark
Bigeye Houndshark
Blackspotted Smoothhound
Blacktip Topeshark or Pencil Shark
Brown Smoothhound
Common Smoothhound
Darksnout or
Deepwater Sicklefin Houndshark
Dusky Smoothhound
Eastern Spotted Gummy Shark
Flapnose Houndshark
Grey Gummy Shark
Grey Smoothhound
Gulf of Mexico Smoothhound
Gummy Shark
Humpback Smoothhound
Japanese Topeshark
Leopard Shark
Longnose Houndshark
Lowfin Houndshark
Narrowfin or Florida Smoothhound
Narrownose Smoothhound
Ocellate Topeshark
Sailback Houndshark
Sharpfin Houndshark
Sharpnose Smoothhound

Sicklefin Houndshark
Sicklefin Smoothhound
Smalleye Smoothhound
Smooth Dogfish
Speckled Smoothhound
Spotless Smoothhound
Spotted Estuary Smoothhound
Spotted Gully Shark or
Sharptooth Houndshark
Starry Smoothhound
Starspotted Smoothhound
Striped Smoothhound or
Striped Dogfish
Tope, Sailfin, or
Soupfin Shark
Venezuelan Dwarf Smoothhound
Western Spotted Gummy Shark
Whiskery Shark
Whitefin Smoothhound
Whitefin Topeshark
Whitespotted Smoothhound
Whitespotted Gummy Shark

*Leopard shark*

# Smoothhounds, Topesharks, Whiskery Sharks, and Other Houndsharks

## Highlights

### ORDER

Groundsharks
*Carcharhiniformes*

### NAME

Houndsharks are named for their habit of hunting in packs.

### SPECIES

There are 46 species in the Houndshark Family and one species in the Barbeled Houndshark Family.

### SIZE

The smallest are about 1 foot long at maturity, and the largest, the spotted houndshark, grows to more than 7 feet long.

### HABITAT

These sharks live in coastal areas in warm and temperate waters throughout the world. Most stay near the ocean floor; none roams the ocean.

Houndsharks are part of the Groundshark Order, the largest order, with more than 270 different species. Other members of the Groundshark Order are catsharks, hammerheads, requiem sharks, and weasel sharks.

Houndsharks are small- to medium-sized sharks with oval eyes that are positioned horizontally on their heads. They have two large dorsal fins and one caudal fin, sharp teeth, and ridges on their heads. Most of them are strong swimmers, especially the topesharks. Many of them swim together in schools, and most in this group are more active at night.

*Triakidae*, the scientific name of this family in the Groundshark Order, is derived from a Greek word meaning "three" and refers to the three-pointed teeth that many houndsharks have.

**H**oundsharks have many of the features of most modern sharks—teeth that are just right for catching and crushing the shellfish that they eat, a nictitating membrane (also called a third eyelid) to protect their eyes, and a well-developed digestive system. Some scientists think that each of the groups in the Houndshark Family—houndsharks, smoothhounds, whiskery sharks, and topesharks— should have its own family, but recent genetic research has confirmed that they belong together.

*Iago houndshark*

## LEOPARD SHARKS

Though many houndsharks and smoothhounds have spots, dots, and stripes, the leopard shark is the most boldly patterned in this group. It is a popular attraction in aquariums because of its distinctive gray and black blotches. Leopard sharks live in shallow waters along the west coast of the United States.

Shark names can be confusing. This shark, known as both a zebra shark and a leopard shark, is in the Carpetshark Order. It's very different from the leopard shark in the Groundshark Order.

## FIN FACT

Male Iago houndsharks are about half the size of the females.

## FISH FOOD

Houndsharks are popular catches for fishing boats because they live in shallow waters and often hang around in large groups. They're not caught as trophies to hang on the wall—eating their meat is common. Commercial fisheries all over the world catch a lot of smoothhounds for people to eat.

The dusky smoothhound (below) has large eyes and a tapered snout. Dusky smoothhounds that live in deep water are often a much darker color than those that live in shallower water, where the sun penetrates. Their coloration helps them camouflage themselves based on the amount of light available where they live.

## SMOOTHHOUNDS

There are more smoothhounds than any other type of houndshark. The scientific name of the smoothhound, *Mustelus*, means "weasel" and refers to their weasel-like snouts. Many of the different smoothhound sharks are similar to one another, and scientists can tell them apart only by checking their vertebrae, which vary among different species.

The goal of most public aquariums is to bring visitors face to face with amazing sharks and other sea creatures so that people learn about them and care about them.

## WHALE SHARKS IN AQUARIUMS

Whale sharks, the biggest sharks in the world, are one of the species that does relatively well in aquariums if they have a big enough exhibit. The first whale sharks were introduced to the public in Japan's Osaka Aquarium Kaiyukan in 2005. Atlanta's Georgia Aquarium is home to four whale sharks: females Alice and Trixie and males Taroko and Yushan. They share a 6.3 million gallon salt water tank, and have all been there for more than six years.

*Whale shark*

*Hammerhead shark*

## SEEING SHARKS IN THE OCEAN

There are places in the world that are particularly good spots to see sharks in their natural settings.

**The warm clear waters of the Bahamas** are some of the best shark diving spots in the world. Divers can swim with dozens of Caribbean reef sharks at a time.

**South Africa** is home to many of the largest species of sharks—such as great white, tiger, and bull sharks—as well as numerous sand tiger sharks.

**Cocos Island, off the coast of Costa Rica,** is a haven for all kinds of marine life, including more than 40 species of sharks. Hammerheads are especially abundant.

**In an area off the southeast coast of the United States known as the "Graveyard of the Atlantic,"** dozens of sharks can be seen gliding past historic shipwrecks.

**Point Reyes Beach, in Northern California**, is known as a hangout for great white sharks, and they can often be seen from the shore for those that don't want an underwater encounter.

Since the first public aquarium opened in London in 1853, people have enjoyed the opportunity to observe creatures of the sea up close. Sharks were included in many early public aquariums, most of them small bottom-dwellers like catsharks and bamboo sharks. In the past few decades, knowledge about what sharks need and how to keep them successfully in aquariums has expanded, and bigger, more diverse collections of sharks have found homes in aquariums around the world.

## ANDY SAYS

Many people first encounter sharks through television shows such as Discovery Channel's "Shark Week." Zoos and aquariums build on that experience by providing a more intimate and close-up meeting. The hope is that people become engaged, perhaps learn to snorkel or dive, and eventually have an encounter in the ocean. With each step, most people's interest in conservation increases and they become more likely to help protect sharks and the oceans. Ultimately we care for what we know, and rarely do people work to protect things they do not care about.

*—Andy Dehart, Marine Biologist*

## WHICH SHARKS THRIVE IN AQUARIUMS?

Sharks in aquariums have a pretty great life. They are fed regularly, don't have to worry about predators, receive regular attention from veterinarians, and are catered to by dedicated aquarists. Although a large percentage of shark species thrive in aquariums, not all do. Some of the first species to be maintained included sand tiger sharks, zebra sharks, catsharks, and bamboo sharks. Horn sharks, bullheads, and Port Jackson sharks are also popular in aquariums because of their strange shapes and relatively small size. Some sharks, such as catsharks and bamboo sharks, even have pups while in aquariums—a sign of successful adaptation.

*Catshark*

*Sand tiger shark*

*Horn shark*

*Leopard shark*

# Shark Training

Some people think of sharks as mindless predators. But researchers and aquarists—people who work with fish—say they are intelligent and capable of learning. Over the past decade, experiments and training exercises in many facilities have proven that sharks are able students.

## RECOGNIZING SOUNDS AND CONTRAST

Aquarists at the Shedd Aquarium in Chicago have been training dolphins and whales for a long time, but they only recently started training sharks. Over a ten-year period, they taught sharks to respond to high-contrast signs: If they put a marker in the water, the sharks swim right up to it, knowing that they will be given food. And they taught sharks to recognize sounds: When they play certain low-frequency sounds, sharks line up to be fed. Aquarist Rachel Wilborn says that she loves working with zebra sharks because they respond well to her touch, and the trained zebra sharks seem to like it when she pats their bellies.

## TRAINING FOR HEALTH

Aquarists at the Pittsburgh PPG Aquarium found it hard to work with some of their sharks, particularly a pair of zebra sharks. The sharks were aggressive and hard to handle, and the workers couldn't get near them to check their health. One of the aquarists, Bob Snowden, started a series of training exercises, rewarding the sharks with food when they allowed themselves to be touched or weighed. The food reward training method works with dogs and other animals, but would it work with sharks? After a few months, the sharks had a change of attitude. Knowing that a reward would be given, they even responded well when they were taken out of the water for brief periods for blood tests and checkups.

## LEARNING EXPERIMENTS

Building on the pioneering work of "shark lady" Eugenie Clark, Managing Director Dr. Tristan Guttridge and researchers at the Biological Field Station in Bimini, in the Bahamas, found that they could teach young lemon sharks to bump a target to get food. But they wanted to find out more about how sharks learn—especially whether they learn from one another. So they studied pairs of lemon sharks. Each pair consisted of one "trained" shark, a shark that had already learned that bumping the target would earn it food, and one that had not been trained. They also tested pairs in which both sharks were untrained. Untrained sharks paired with trained sharks usually learned to hit the target more quickly than those in untrained pairs. The researchers concluded that the sharks learned from each other.

Zebra sharks respond well to training at the Shedd Arboretum in Chicago and the Pittsburgh PPG Aquarium.

## ANDY SAYS

The most rewarding part of my career has been working with the same sharks day in and day out. When working with these sharks, it is clear that individuals, even sharks of the same species, have unique behaviors. Some of my favorite experiences have been seeing the sharks that I have worked with learn new behaviors. Sharks in aquariums are certainly not domesticated animals, but it is both possible and rewarding for aquarists to build relationships with the sharks and other animals they care for. Sharks are far more intelligent than most people think and this is another reason why I care so deeply about their survival.

—*Andy Dehart,*
*Marine Biologist*

## BLINKING

Dr. Samuel ("Doc") Gruber, a pioneer in shark research and training, was one of the first scientists to conduct experiments on how sharks learn. He started working at the Mote Marine Laboratory in Sarasota, Florida, where he studied lemon sharks. In one of his first experiments, he taught the lemon sharks to blink at a flash of light. He says that they learned to do this about ten times faster than cats do. "Doc" Gruber has been working with sharks for more than 40 years. His more recent experiments observe how sharks learn to avoid fishing hooks and magnetic fields.

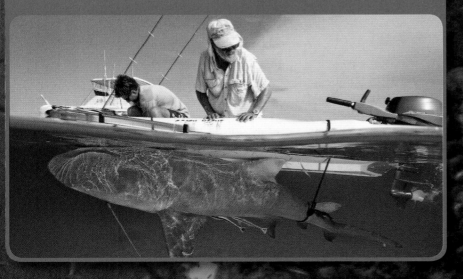

When "Doc" Gruber was a teenager, a huge hammerhead shark appeared before him while he was swimming. He says, "The giant fish was beautiful, magnificent, and was circling me. When he did not actually kill and consume me, I knew that I wanted to learn more about these splendid creatures."

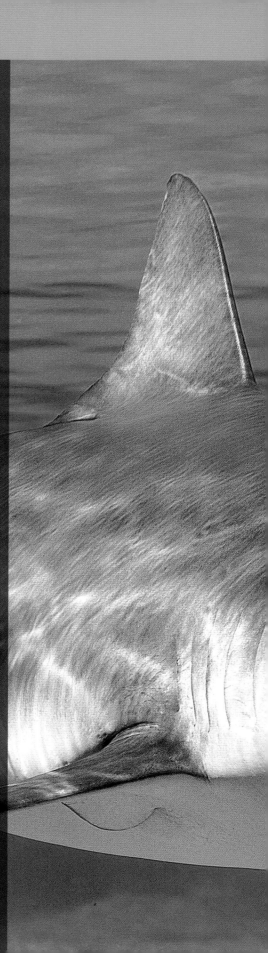

**REQUIEM SHARKS**
*Carcharhinidae*

Atlantic Sharpnose Shark
Australian Blacktip Shark
Australian Sharpnose Shark
Bignose Shark
Bizant River Shark
Blacknose Shark
Blackspot Shark
Blacktip Shark
Blacktip Shark
Blue Shark
Borneo River Shark
Borneo Shark
Brazilian Sharpnose Shark
Broadfin Shark
Bronze Whaler
Bull Shark
Caribbean Reef Shark
Caribbean Sharpnose Shark
Creek Whaler
Daggernose Shark
Dusky Shark
False Smalltail Shark
Finetooth Shark
Galapagos Shark
Ganges Shark
Graceful Shark
Grey Reef Shark
Grey Sharpnose Shark

Hardnose Shark
Irrawaddy River Shark
Java or Pigeye Shark
Lemon Shark
Milk Shark
Nervous Shark
New Guinea River Shark
Night Shark
Oceanic Whitetip Shark
Pacific Sharpnose Shark
Pondicherry Shark
Sandbar Shark
Sharptooth Lemon Shark
Silky Shark
Silvertip Shark
Sliteye Shark
Smalltail Shark
Smoothtooth Shark
Spadenose Sharpnose Shark
Speartooth Shark
Spinner Shark
Spottail Shark
Tiger Shark
Whitecheek Shark
Whitenose Shark
Whitetip Reef Shark

# Requiem Sharks

**M**any of the best-known sharks—the ones we see the most and the ones that are most abundant in the ocean—are requiem sharks. Some of them are aggressive hunters, including bull, tiger, and oceanic whitetip sharks. All are good swimmers, with strong bodies and long fins. Some requiem sharks, particularly the oceanic whitetips, are loners. Others are social and spend time with each other, sometimes teaming up to catch prey or to ward off attackers. Some requiem sharks, particularly lemon sharks, seem to like hanging out together.

Requiem sharks have the usual groundshark features: small eyes, nictitating membranes (third eyelids), and fins behind their gills.

*Bull shark*

## Highlights

### ORDER

Groundsharks
*Carcharhinidae*

### NAME

The name requiem comes from the French word for shark, *requin*.

### SPECIES

54 species in one family

### SIZE

Most are medium to large, growing to 9 to 10 feet long. The tiger shark can grow to 18 feet long. The smallest, such as the Borneo shark and the Australian sharpnose, are just over 2 feet long.

### HABITAT

They live in warm and temperate waters all over the world.

Requiem sharks are part of the Groundshark Order, the largest shark order. Other members of the Groundshark Order are catsharks, hammerheads, houndsharks, and weasel sharks.

Caribbean, grey, blacktip, and whitetip reef sharks are named for their habit of visiting reefs. Some live in the Caribbean Sea and the Gulf of Mexico; most live in the Indian and Pacific oceans. They are usually 4 to 7 feet long and like shallow water, where they find and eat small fish and shellfish. They often join in feeding frenzies, where dozens or even hundreds of sharks compete for prey.

## CAVE OF THE SLEEPING SHARKS

The strong current running through this cave on the coast of Mexico allows reef sharks to take a rest. It pushes water over their gills, allowing them to absorb oxygen from the water without constantly swimming. Divers report that there are sometimes more than 20 sharks "sleeping" in the cave at the same time.

## WHITETIP REEF SHARKS

have strong cheek muscles, which allow them to force water from their cheeks over their gills to get oxygen when they rest. They hunt at night, often in groups.

## BLACKTIP REEF SHARKS

are easy to spot—the black tip on each fin gives them away. Most of them choose a spot with an ample food supply and stay near it, not wandering far to hunt.

## CARIBBEAN REEF SHARKS

are the biggest of the group, sometimes growing up to 10 feet. They are especially good at hearing low-frequency sounds, which alert them to the presence of fish swimming nearby.

## GREY REEF SHARKS

are fast swimmers and the most aggressive of the reef sharks. They make an impressive threat display, dropping their pectoral fins and hunching their shoulders before they attack.

Oceanic whitetips have hard lives. They live in the open ocean and need to keep swimming every moment of their lives in order to breathe. Luckily, they have huge, strong fins that allow them to glide through the ocean day and night searching for schools of fish to feast on. Most are less than 10 feet long and occupy deep waters in all the temperate regions of the world.

## GUESS WHAT?

Jacques Cousteau, the famous oceanographer, called oceanic whitetips "the most dangerous sharks in the ocean" because they are so efficient at tracking down and feeding on shipwreck survivors.

**Strong fins**

## SHIPWRECK SHARKS

There isn't a lot of food in the open ocean so oceanic whitetips take advantage of any opportunity to eat, sometimes finding a decent meal only once a month. When they hear or sense a shipwreck, they spring into action. Unfortunately for survivors of shipwrecks, whitetips looking for something good to eat will take a bite out of sailors and passengers who land in the water.

One of the most famous and deadly shipwreck-and-shark incidents features the oceanic whitetip. During World War II, the British troopship HMS *Nova Scotia* was sunk by torpedoes from a German submarine off the coast of South Africa, casting about 900 people into the shark-infested waters. Hundreds died, many from drowning and exposure, but oceanic whitetip sharks took lives as well.

Oceanic whitetip sharks are loners, but sometimes allow pilot fish and dolphin fish to accompany them.

## FIN FACT

Because their fins are large, oceanic whitetip sharks are caught for shark fin soup. Overfishing has led to a dramatic decline in their numbers—researchers estimate that their population has declined by more than 70 percent in the past few decades. Oceanic whitetips are considered Critically Endangered—the most serious designation before extinction—in the Atlantic by the International Union for the Conservation of Nature, and conservationists are hoping to make it illegal to capture them so that the species does not become extinct.

# Lemon Sharks

The lemon shark has light brown skin tinged with yellow, which camouflages it well on the sandy ocean floor. Their name also applies to the little indentations that make their skin look and feel like lemon rind. Lemon sharks usually stay in fairly shallow water, up to 300 feet deep, and are most commonly found in the Caribbean. They average 8 to 9 feet in length, and eat smaller sharks, seabirds, turtles, crustaceans, and stingrays.

## COOPERATIVE SHARKS

Lemon sharks are known as the lab rats of the shark world, and they are often used in experiments that test the hearing, vision, and intelligence of sharks. Although they are large and considered aggressive, they seem to thrive in aquarium conditions and cooperate with researchers.

## ANDY SAYS

I can tell you that individual sharks of numerous species have distinct personality traits, just as individual dogs or cats do. The problem is setting up experimental conditions that can catch this.

—Andy Dehart, Marine Biologist

## FRIENDLY LEMONS

Lemon sharks are social and spend time with each other. In groups, they tend to stay with sharks of the same size. Because they interact with each other and do well in tanks, they are good candidates for behavior studies and experiments. When trying to determine whether sharks learn behaviors from other sharks, scientists have observed that young lemon sharks seem to pick up social cues from those with more experience. Trainers who work with lemon sharks say they seem to prefer each other's company to staying alone.

## SHARK PERSONALITY

Researchers at the Bimini Biological Research Center are trying to determine whether individual sharks have specific personality traits. They are following tagged lemon shark specimens—both in captivity and in the wild—to see if they swim faster or slower, react to people and other fish around them, and behave in specific ways.

**B**lue sharks have big eyes; elegant long fins; and beautiful, sleek, dark blue bodies.  Their snouts, which are called rostrums, are cone-shaped, giving them streamlined bodies that help them swim fast. Their long tails and oarlike pectoral fins also speed them up. Blue sharks are usually 10 to 12 feet long and are found in the open ocean worldwide, in temperate and tropical waters.

## COOL-WATER BLUES

Blue sharks like cool water. When the water gets too warm for them in summer months, they migrate to cooler waters. Tagged blue sharks have been tracked migrating from New York to Brazil, traveling a distance of 3,740 miles.

**Blue sharks following yellowfin tuna.**

## BIG EATERS

Blue sharks eat a lot. They will follow a school of small fish, such as anchovies or sardines, and gorge. Sometimes they will then vomit and start eating again.

When they digest their food, the portion that they don't need for energy right away is stored in their bodies for several days or even weeks— overeating allows them to survive and keep swimming even if they can't find food for a while.

### DID YOU KNOW?

Male blue sharks let females know they are interested in mating by biting them—hard. This is true of many shark species, and females develop tough skin so that they can tolerate these bites. Female blue sharks have been especially successful at this skin-toughening tactic—their skin is three times the thickness of male blue sharks.

# Bull Sharks

There is nothing delicate or dainty about bull sharks. They are heavy and aggressive sharks, with a forceful bite. When hunting, they "bump and bite": They stun their prey with a hard push with their massive snouts, then eat them. Bull sharks have high levels of hormones that cause aggression, and they are credited with one of the highest rates of bites on humans—just behind great whites. They are not very long, usually under 10 feet, but inch for inch bull sharks are considered to have the most powerful bite of any shark. They live in warm, shallow waters all over the world.

**BITS & BITES**

One of the reasons that bull sharks are so dangerous is that they swim in places where many people swim—shallow waters and fresh water.

**FIN FACT**

After Hurricane Katrina, bull sharks were found in Lake Pontchartrain.

## FRESH WATER SHARKS

Bulls are among the few sharks that can live in fresh as well as salt water. They can do this because they are able to balance the amount of salt in their bodies with the salinity of the water they're swimming in. Bull sharks don't make a decision to do this—their bodies react automatically to the amount of salt in the water.

Bull sharks have been found in the Mississippi River as far north as Illinois, and at least 1,000 miles up the Amazon. Lake Nicaragua is full of bulls, known there as Nicaragua sharks.

Bull sharks have small eyes. But they spend much of their time in murky waters—such as the mouths of rivers and shallow ocean waters—where vision would not help them much.

## FIN FACT

The bull shark is territorial and will attack anything that enters its territory. Most sharks and other fish won't attack animals larger than they are, but bull sharks will attack when threatened.

**ANDY SAYS**

Bull sharks' poor eyesight may explain why there are so many recorded bites on humans. They rely on senses other than vision, which sometimes makes them think that people are their regular prey.
—*Andy Dehart, Marine Biologist*

# Tiger Sharks

Tiger sharks are one of the most voracious eaters in the ocean. They live in temperate waters all over the world and can be found in both coastal waters and the open seas. One of the only places where they are not found is the Mediterranean. They swim in waters down to 450 feet deep. Tiger sharks usually hunt alone, swimming closer to the surface at night to feed in shallower waters. Their main diet is bony fish, shellfish, and sea turtles.

## TUMMY TROUBLES

When a shark eats food that doesn't agree with it, it can evert, or vomit up, its whole stomach, turning it inside out and pushing out whatever it can't digest. The shark then swallows the stomach and pushes it back into place.

Tiger sharks do this often. They feed on the meat of sea turtles, but can't digest the large shells and need to get rid of them.

**Sea turtle**

## STOMACH CONTENTS

Tiger sharks are known as "garbage guts" and will eat almost anything. They have large, curved, pointy teeth that can puncture whatever comes their way, including metal. Large, inedible objects—including parts of cars—have been found in tiger shark stomachs.

Items found in one tiger shark's stomach included a doll, a can of ham, and several beer bottles.

Horse, pig, and crocodile heads have been found in tiger shark stomachs.

Tiger sharks are named for the stripes on their backs. These stripes are easy to see in young tiger sharks, but they fade as the sharks grow older and are barely visible in mature sharks.

Metal objects, including license plates, nails, and oil cans, have been eaten by tiger sharks.

Some items that seem too big to fit in a tiger shark, like tires, have been found in their stomachs.

Tiger sharks have big sharp teeth that can rip through nearly anything.

# Tiger Traits

## GUESS WHAT?

Sharks play a role in the history and mythology of Hawaii and the native Hawaiian culture. Tiger sharks are not only considered sacred, but legend has it that tiger shark eyeballs have special powers.

Tiger sharks are sneaky. They generally swim slowly, almost sluggishly, and seem to be ignoring the fish around them. But they can turn quickly and attack with great speed when they have spotted their prey.

## ANDY SAYS

My experience with tiger sharks has led me to believe they are quite intelligent and capable of learning. At one dive destination in the Bahamas, there have been several interactions between tiger sharks and humans. At this site, the same individual sharks return repeatedly, and it is one of the places where you clearly see individual traits for each animal.

—*Andy Dehart, Marine Biologist*

# Duskies and Silkies

**S**ilky sharks have slender bodies with delicate, curved fins and skin that is metallic silver on top and white below. They are called "silky" because their dermal denticles (toothlike scales) are close together, which makes their skin smooth. Silky sharks grow to about 8 feet long and they are commonly found in the open ocean in temperate waters all over the world.

**Dusky sharks** are also known as bronze whalers and copper sharks for their light metallic skin color. These fast-swimming sharks often hunt in groups, and cooperate in finding and catching prey. They sometimes follow big schools of fish, such as the huge sardine runs that occur off the coast of Africa.

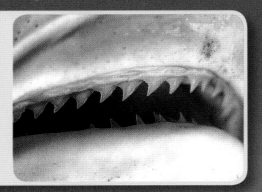

Dusky sharks have lower teeth that are straight and pointy, which help them grab on to prey. Their upper teeth are broad and triangular, and help them tear meat into pieces small enough to swallow.

Dusky sharks swim for long distances. In summer they head for cool waters, and in winter they return to temperate regions. But females return to the region where they themselves were born when it is time to give birth to pups.

**FIN FACT**

Silky shark pups are born live, usually in a protected place such as a reef or continental shelf. They stay there for several months and don't set out for the open ocean until they are much bigger.

Silky sharks follow schools of fish such as the tuna shown here. They are often accidentally scooped up as bycatch in fishing nets used by commercial fishing boats that are looking for tuna.

**S**pinner sharks have an interesting way of catching prey. When they find a school of small fish, they charge up through the school, snapping on all sides until they catch a fish. They then swallow the fish whole because their teeth are not shaped for tearing prey apart. Spinners can be very entertaining. Their speed when they move upward to catch prey sometimes propels them right out of the water. When they jump out of the water they spin, sometimes doing three or four turns before diving under again. Spinner sharks often hang around in groups, putting on spectacular shows for those lucky enough to see them.

**Sandbar sharks** are found on sandbars in shallow water near coastlines in temperate climates. Their skin is a bronze-brown color, sometimes with a blue or gray tone; their underbellies are pale. Sandbar sharks like to stay in warm water. In the summer, they will live as far north as New England, but in winter they move south to Florida and Mexico.

## BITS & BITES
Sandbar sharks can cruise along the ocean floor because their big, triangular dorsal fins give them stability.

*Spinner sharks, like the one shown here, propel out of the water at high speed and are rarely captured in mid-flight because they move so fast. If only they would stop and pose for the camera!*

The Atlantic sharpnose shark is one of a group of sharpnose sharks that are named for their long, pointed snouts.

# Learning from Sharks

Shark research takes many forms. Research into deep sea-dwelling sharks can be conducted with modern deep-diving equipment. Tagging experiments allow researchers to follow shark movements and migration patterns. And research in laboratories enables scientists to examine sharks inside and out.

## MEDICAL RESEARCH

Sharks get viruses and cancerous tumors just like other animals, but they have low rates of disease and strong immune systems. Scientists are studying shark immune systems to see if there are lessons to be learned about how sharks fight disease that can be applied to disease prevention in people. A study at the Georgetown University Medical Center found that squalamine, a molecule found in dogfish sharks, may kill some human viruses. Although researchers are still studying its side effects, squalamine is already being used as an antibiotic and is being tested as a drug to treat eye diseases and lung cancer.

There is other medical research being done to see if shark skin can be used in grafts for people with serious burns. And scientists are studying a compound in shark blood that stops clots from forming to see if this can help people with heart disease.

## SURVIVAL OF THE SPECIES

One important topic for shark research is how many of each type of shark live in a region and when these sharks give birth to pups. This information is critical to fishery management, a process meant to control the number of sharks that fishing boats are allowed to bring in. If the boats harvest a particular shark species faster than members of that species are able to reproduce, the species will eventually die out. If the sharks are taken after they have had pups instead of before, that helps keep populations healthy, so it is important to collect data about these subjects.

People have been fascinated with sharks for a long time, and there has been a lot of research done on them over the years. It is hard to gather data about creatures that live in the ocean, but new technology is making it easier to learn more about sharks, their feeding habits, travel patterns, and other important topics.

## DID YOU KNOW?

Because of the complicated patterns of dermal denticles (toothlike projections) on shark skin, it's hard for anything—including bacteria—to grow on it. Scientists are studying shark skin to see if it can be used to prevent or cure bacterial infections in humans.

# Tagging

One of the tools that shark experts use in their research is tagging, which involves capturing a shark, inserting a small tag into its skin, and then releasing it. Some tags are electronic and record information that is analyzed when the tagged shark is captured at a future time. Other tags "ping"—that is, they transmit signals that let the researchers know where the shark is, and they may transmit other information as well.

## SHARK LIVES

Many shark experts specialize in one type of shark and gather huge amounts of information about it. Dr. Jennifer Schmidt of the University of Illinois in Chicago studies whale shark DNA and tracks their travels using GPS tracking systems. Knowing their migration patterns will help scientists devise strategies to keep the population healthy. Scientists at the Seattle Aquarium have been keeping tabs on a group of bluntnose sixgill sharks in Puget Sound. They've found that the sixgills feed in odd ways, sometimes standing on their heads while they eat their favorite foods. Sometimes, they're surprised at what they learn. For example, sixgills seem to prefer rotten salmon to fresh bait.

## NOAA

The National Oceanic and Atmospheric Administration has an extensive tagging program. This program is a cooperative effort between the National Marine Fisheries Service and people engaged in professional and recreational fishing. Through this program, more than 220,000 sharks in 52 species have been tagged, and more than 13,000 of these sharks have been recaptured so the data in their tags can be studied. One sandbar shark was captured after wearing a tag for 27 years. A blue shark was tracked over a distance of 3,900 miles. Tagging helps experts identify the age and population of shark species, and this information helps them determine the number of fish that can be safely harvested.

**1** Catching the shark

**2** Bringing it on board in a cradle

**3** Working on it

**4** Attaching the tag

**5** Releasing it

# WORKING WITH SHARKS

For people who love sharks and would like to have a career that involves working with them, there are many ways to do so. There are jobs for people with different talents, abilities, and education levels who want to work with these magnificent animals every day.

"Marine biologist" is a general term that covers many scientists who work in watery environments. **Marine biologists** study the ocean and the plants and animals that live in it. They take courses in college that teach them about water quality, ways of monitoring the health of fish (including sharks), and the anatomy of all kinds of creatures that live in the seas. There are many jobs related to sharks that marine biologists can do, including tagging, monitoring shark populations, working in aquariums, and finding new shark species.

**Icthyologists** (ick-thee-AH-low-jists) are scientists who study fish. Specialists study sharks' health and physiology. Some icthyologists work in laboratories, some teach in universities. They often join research missions. In general, most individuals working in the research side have a master's or doctoral degree in marine science.

**Aquarists** work in aquariums and manage tanks and exhibits. Usually, they are responsible for feeding sharks and maintaining water quality and filtration systems. Sometimes, they train sharks as well. A degree in marine biology and diving certification is often necessary for a job as an aquarist, but many aquariums offer volunteer and internship opportunities to help students get started.

**Divers and photographers.** Dive operators hire divers to take people on tours to see sharks. Certification in diving and knowledge about shark behavior is needed to do this safely. Some divers specialize in underwater photography and take incredible photographs of sharks, such as the ones in this book.

**Conservation biologists** work with environmental groups or government agencies to promote conservation measures for sharks. Many in this field have higher degrees in marine science, but others have degrees in environmental policy or law.

**8**
**SPECIES**

**WEASEL SHARKS**
*Hemigaleidae*

Atlantic Weasel Shark
Australian Weasel Shark
Hooktooth Shark
Sicklefin Weasel Shark
Slender Weasel Shark
Snaggletooth Shark
Straighttooth Weasel Shark
Whitetip Weasel Shark

*Sicklefin weasel shark*

# Weasel Sharks

## Highlights

### ORDER

Groundsharks
*Carcharhiniformes*

### NAME

Weasel sharks are
named for their
tapered snout, which
looks very much like
that of a weasel.

### SPECIES

Eight species in
one family.

### SIZE

Most weasel sharks
are between 3 and
4 feet long, but the
snaggletooth shark
grows to over 8 feet long.

### HABITAT

Weasel sharks live in
shallow coastal waters
all over the world.

Weasel sharks are part
of the Groundshark
Order, the largest
order, with more than
270 different species.
Other members of
the Groundshark
Order are catsharks,
hammerheads,
houndsharks, and
requiem sharks.

Like most groundsharks, weasel sharks have small oval eyes on the sides of their heads and nictitating membranes protecting their eyes. Their tail fins have strong lobes and wavy edges. Some species, such as the snaggletooth and Atlantic weasel sharks, are specialist feeders—their diet is mainly cephalopods like octopuses and squid, though they also eat some small bony fish. There are a few species that are confined to specific areas, including the whitetip weasel shark, which lives only in a small area off the coast of South Africa.

The fast-swimming snaggletooth shark has a slender body that is tapered at both ends, with a long tail. This body shape helps it swim quickly. Their skin color is light gray or bronze, with no markings. Snaggletooth sharks live in the western Pacific Ocean and the Red Sea, but are so rarely seen that they are thought to be nearly extinct. When spotted, they are usually found in water that is about 300 feet deep.

The snaggletooth's teeth help it catch its main prey. The teeth on their top jaw are sharp and serrated, which allows the snaggletooth to trap and pierce the slippery octopuses and squid it likes to eat. The bottom teeth are hooked, which make them well suited for tearing up prey.

## FIN FACT

In many species of sharks the females are larger than the males, but male snaggletooth sharks are about twice the size of the females.

A snaggletooth is a tooth that is crooked or sticks out. All the sharks in this group have teeth that are wickedly sharp for such small sharks.

The snaggletooth shark is little known and rarely seen, but it is a member of a prehistoric genus. An ancient relative of the snaggletooth, *hemiprestis serra*, left many large teeth behind. Based on the size of the teeth, scientists estimate that *hemiprestis serra* was about 12 feet long.

The weasel shark, shown at left, has a snout that looks like the nose of a weasel, which is shown on the right.

Virginie Abrial was surprised and excited to see a rare snaggletooth shark on one of her dives in Sharm-el-Sheikh, Egypt. The shark came straight toward her, its body moving with a wavy motion. She described its mouth as "fearsome, with big teeth."

*Virginie Abrial's video of her snaggletooth encounter*

# Why Are Sharks in Trouble?

Species disappear all the time because of natural causes. In the shark world, some 2,000 species have existed since prehistoric times and those that couldn't adapt to new conditions vanished, while new species appeared. These changes took place over millions of years. But much more recent changes in the health of the oceans and of fish populations around the world have resulted in shrinking shark populations, causing growing concerns.

The United Nations Food and Agriculture Organization estimates that almost half of shark species have suffered serious declines in population, and about 20 percent of these are in danger of extinction. This is not happening over millions of years, but much more rapidly—over just the past 100 years—and scientists point to several causes.

- **Global Warming** Increases in the production and use of fossil fuels (like oil and coal) is warming up the air and ocean waters, making it harder for sharks and the fish they feed on to survive.

- **Shrinking Habitats** Shark habitats like coral reefs and continental shelves are being damaged and destroyed by human activity and global warming.

- **Pollution** Pesticides and fertilizers used on land can run off into waterways and, along with oil spills from ships and drilling accidents, can make areas uninhabitable by fish, reducing the amount of food available to sharks.

- **Population Growth** The number of people on earth has more than doubled in the past 50 years, meaning greater consumption of fossil fuels, more fishing, and fewer fish for sharks to eat.

- **Overfishing** As commercial fishing boats have become more mechanized—using huge nets, lines, and trawls to scoop fish from the sea in one big sweep—they can harvest enormous quantities of fish on a single outing. Sharks can be caught in the nets, where they die because they cannot breathe.

- **Finning** The most desirable part of the shark in some parts of the world is the fin, used for the delicacy known as shark fin soup. Some fishing operations cut off the fins at sea and throw the rest of the shark back in the water, where the shark drowns (because sharks can't swim without fins). Sharks with large fins—such as oceanic whitetips and great hammerheads—are prime targets for finning and are now listed by the International Union for the Conservation of Nature as vulnerable. Of the estimated 70 million sharks killed each year, more than a third are killed just for their fins.

Sharks have been swimming in the ocean since before dinosaurs roamed the earth, and—while dinosaurs have died out—sharks have survived and thrived. This is because they evolved and adapted over the past 400 million years, developing sharper senses and features like replaceable teeth, jaws that thrust forward, and dermal denticles that protect their skin.

Sharks are a vital part of the ocean ecosystem. They are apex predators, which means they control the populations of the smaller fish in the sea. Without sharks, or with too few sharks, the fine balance will be lost—smaller fish populations will grow uncontrolled, and then they will run out of prey and start to die off.

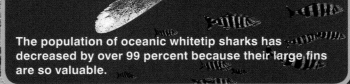

The population of oceanic whitetip sharks has decreased by over 99 percent because their large fins are so valuable.

# Hope for the Future

Rather than being afraid of sharks, people should be afraid for sharks, as their populations are seriously threatened. Scientists, legislators, and advocates—people who love sharks—are working to protect sharks in many ways.

## HELPING SHARKS

There are many things people can do to help sharks have a healthy future, from choosing not to eat shark fin soup to contacting their government representatives to encourage them to pass laws to help protect sharks. To get more involved, start by letting people know that sharks are important and that they're endangered. Talk to teachers about sharks and encourage them to get their classes involved in learning more about sharks. Share this book with friends and family. For more ways to get involved and learn about sharks, see the Resources section at the end of this book.

**Education** One way to protect sharks is through education, making as many people as possible aware that we need sharks in the world. Sharks have a reputation for being dangerous killers, when in fact they are rarely dangerous to people. People learn about the importance of sharks through books like this one, television programs, and shark exhibits in aquariums.

**Legislation** Another way to keep shark populations healthy is through legislation. Laws have been passed to limit practices that kill so many sharks. In 2010, Hawaii banned the sale of shark fins, and shark protection laws have been passed in California, Oregon, and Washington as well.

**Conservation** Conservationists are working to protect reefs, pupping grounds (places where sharks go to give birth), and other places where sharks live. They are funding research to figure out what is hurting these regions and how to stop and reverse the damage, including ways to slow down global warming by reducing the amount of energy we use.

**Maintaining Sanctuaries** Huge shark sanctuaries have been set up as safe havens for sharks, places where no fishing takes place and where pupping grounds are protected. The first such sanctuary was set up in 2009 by Palau, a Pacific island that bans all shark fishing to protect the 135 species of sharks and skates that live in the 230,000 square miles of water around the island. Another major haven is the Raja Ampat Sanctuary in Indonesia, where new laws passed in 2013 protect sharks in the coastal and ocean waters around the island. In the United States, the National Oceanic and Atmospheric Administration has established an Apex Predator Program that includes 14 sanctuaries protecting sharks and other endangered fish in more than 150,000 square miles of water, from the Great Lakes to coastal regions.

**9 SPECIES**

**HORN SHARKS
AND BULLHEAD SHARKS**
*Heterodontidae*

*Port Jackson shark*

# Horn Sharks and Bullhead Sharks

## Highlights

### ORDER

Horn sharks
and Bullhead sharks
*Heterodontiformes*

### NAME

Bullheads and horn sharks get their names from the unusually shaped, hard, and hornlike ridges on their heads.

### SPECIES

There are nine sharks in this order.

### SIZE

Most bullheads and horn sharks average about 2 feet long; some grow to as much as 5 feet long; and Port Jackson sharks can grow to 8 feet long.

### HABITAT

These sharks live in warm and tropical shallow waters near the coasts of the Indian and Pacific oceans.

Horn sharks and bullhead sharks have a distinctive look. Their mouths are pushed forward in front of their eyes, they have trumpet-shaped nostrils, distinct ridges that connect their nostrils to their mouths and run along their backs, and they have venomous spines near their dorsal fins. They are not very active and usually eat small creatures that are nearby on the ocean floor.

# Slow Movers

**B**ullheads are known for their sluggishness, especially during the day. They eat small fish, worms, and crustaceans found nearby. Because they are slow and tend to stay in one place, they are sometimes eaten by other creatures, including other sharks. They live in shallow waters, where they can be prey to eagles and seals. Bullheads and horn sharks do have some advantages: Their spines are toxic, their horns are sharp, and predators sometimes spit them out or stop biting long enough for the sharks to get away.

*Galapagos bullhead shark*

# A TOOTH FOR EVERY TASK

*Horn shark*

The horn shark has different kinds of teeth in its mouth and uses them in different ways. But before it starts using its teeth, the bullhead uses its mouth like a suction tube to suck in prey. Then its sharp front teeth pin the prey into position. The flat side teeth crush and grind the prey into smaller, easy-to-swallow pieces.

*Port Jackson shark*

Bullheads, like most sharks, don't raise their young, but they take great care where they lay their egg cases. They find safe places between rocks and under ledges, and wedge in the egg cases securely so that they are not easily broken or eaten by other fish during the year they take to hatch. Port Jackson sharks, like the one at left, gather to place the cases together in safe, protected places. They seem to remember these places, returning to them year after year to lay their eggs.

# Extreme Sharks

Sometimes, a single shark in a species grows bigger, stays smaller, or swims faster than the rest of the members of its species. Here are some maximums and averages.

## TEN BIGGEST SHARKS IN THE WORLD

This list shows the maximum and average sizes for each of the ten biggest sharks recorded by scientists. The list changes all the time, as bigger sharks are observed or caught and as more data is collected. There may be bigger sharks out there, but these are very big sharks.

### 1. Whale shark
*Maximum: 65.6 feet; Average: 23 feet*

### 2. Basking shark
*Maximum: 29.5 feet; Average: 21.7 feet*

### 3. Pacific sleeper shark
*Maximum: 23 feet; Average: 13.1 feet*

### 4. Greenland shark
*Maximum: 22 feet; Average: 10.5 feet*

### 5. Great white shark
*Maximum: 20.2 feet; Average: 14.2 feet*

### 6. Common thresher shark
*Maximum: 20.1 feet; Average: 11.2 feet*

### 7. Great hammerhead
*Maximum: 19 feet; Average: 8.6 feet*

### 8. Megamouth shark
*Maximum: 18 feet; Average: 14.8 feet*

### 9. Tiger shark
*Maximum: 18 feet; Average: 9.2 feet*

### 10. Goblin shark
*Maximum: 16.4 feet; Average: 9.8 feet*

Biggest, smallest, fastest, strongest—for sharks, it's just their nature to grow and move as quickly as they can.

## TEN SMALLEST SHARKS DISCOVERED

1. **Dwarf lanternshark**
   *6.7 inches*
2. **Pale catshark**
   *8.3 inches*
3. **Smalleye pygmy shark**
   *8.7 inches*
4. **Panama ghost catshark**
   *9.1 inches*
5. **Green lanternshark**
   *9.1 inches*
6. **Shorttail lanternshark**
   *9.4 inches*
7. **African lanternshark**
   *9.4 inches*
8. **Spined pygmy shark**
   *9.8 inches*
9. **Atlantic ghost catshark**
   *9.8 inches*
10. **Broadnose catshark**
    *10.2 inches*

## BIGGEST TAIL
**Common thresher** Up to 52 percent of body size, 12 feet long, 800 pounds

## BIGGEST TEETH
**Great white shark**
Up to 2 inches long

## BIGGEST MOUTH
**Whale shark**
Up to 15 feet wide

## THICKEST SKIN
**Whale shark**
Up to 3½ inches thick

## BIGGEST EYES
**Bigeye thresher shark** Up to 7 inches high. Biggest by proportion of any vertebrate other than birds. (If a 5-foot-tall person had eyes this big, each would be 2½ inches wide.)

# Performance Records

If there were a shark Olympics, these sharks would be gold medalists. They can't be judged the same way swimmers and ice skaters are, but researchers have ingenious machines and experiments to measure a shark's performance.

## FASTEST

The salmon shark was clocked by the U.S. Navy at 55 miles per hour. Previously, the shortfin mako, which had been clocked at 44 miles per hour, was considered the fastest.

*Salmon shark*

*Mako shark*

## DEEPEST-DIVING

A Portuguese dogfish was found 12,000 feet below the surface during a study of deep-sea fish. These sharks spend most of their time below 1,200 feet, but the 12,000-foot-deep waters are probably not where it spends all its time.

## LONGEST MIGRATION

A great white shark named Nicole migrated from Africa to Australia and back—a journey of over 12,000 miles—in nine months. Her epic migration was recorded with a tracking device.

## BEST HEARING

The silky shark has responded to low-frequency sounds from ¼ mile away.

# LIFE CYCLE RECORDS

Researchers gather as much data about shark life spans and birth records as they can—but it's difficult to get exact numbers because sharks don't fill out questionnaires.

## MOST SHARK PUPS IN A SINGLE LITTER

*Live birth:* blue shark, 135 pups.
*From eggs stored in a female shark's body:* whale shark, 300 eggs (in a whale shark captured in 1996).

## SMALLEST WHALE SHARK PUP

15 inches long—but they grow to more than 40 feet by adulthood.

## SMALLEST PUP

The pups of the dwarf lanternshark are under 2½ inches long.

## SHORTEST PREGNANCY

Bonnetheads give birth to live pups that hatch from eggs stored in the mother's belly after five months of pregnancy.

## LONGEST PREGNANCY

The spiny dogfish is pregnant for about two years. Right now, that is the longest confirmed shark pregnancy on record. It is also one of the longest pregnancies of any animal—only the black alpine salamander's is longer, at three years in cold climates. But scientists are investigating evidence that other sharks, including the frilled sharks, may be pregnant for three and a half years or more. For now, the spiny dogfish holds the record for longest pregnancy among sharks.

## LONGEST-LIVED SHARK

Scientists think the Greenland shark can live more than 200 years, based on its rate of growth, but they haven't yet found a way to prove this.

Blue shark

Bonnethead shark

Greenland shark

## 15 SPECIES

*Great white shark*

# Mackerel Sharks

## Highlights

### ORDER

Mackerel sharks
*Lamniformes*

### NAME

Mackerel sharks eat
a lot of mackerel, a
small bony fish, and
are named after them.

### SPECIES

There are 15 species
of mackerel sharks
in seven families.

### SIZE

Mostly large sharks.
The biggest is the
basking shark, which
grows to almost 30
feet; the smallest is
the crocodile shark,
which rarely grows to
more than 3½ feet.

### HABITAT

Wide-ranging, ocean-
roaming sharks. Many
prefer warm waters, but
some, such as salmon
sharks, can survive in
icy waters. Some swim
near the coastline in
shallow water; others
are deep-sea sharks and
live down to 3,000 feet
beneath the surface.

This is one of the oldest groups of sharks—many of its members have existed, in close to their current form, for over 120 million years. Mackerel sharks have big mouths that extend behind their eyes. Most are warm blooded, which means that they can raise their body temperature to adjust to the water temperature. This gives them extra speed, and the fastest swimmers in the shark world are mackerels. Mackerel sharks roll their eyes back in their sockets to protect them when they feed.

Some of the most familiar sharks—the great whites, makos, and threshers—fall within this group. So do some unusual deep-sea sharks, such as goblins, crocodile sharks, and megamouths.

# Thresher Sharks

The thresher shark gets its name from the way its tail resembles a farming tool used to thresh grain. Thresher sharks whip their tails back and forth in the water to stun the fish that they like to eat. They are big sharks, and the common thresher and the bigeye thresher are among the 20 largest sharks in the world.

## BIG TAILS

Thresher tails can grow to half of their body length, and make up a third of their weight. Threshers use their tails as weapons. When they find a school of fish, they whip their tails around vigorously. When the fish are stunned and trapped, the threshers begin to eat.

Although their long tails are useful to threshers, they can get caught in nets and lines that are used by fishing boats to scoop up big hauls of fish. When the lines and nets are hoisted up, the threshers hang upside down from their tails and die because they can't breathe out of water. Bycatch—accidental capture of fish in nets and on lines that are after other fish—is a huge problem for all sharks, but threshers are particularly hurt by it.

## FIN FACT

Thresher sharks can jump right out of the water. This is called breaching, and while no one knows exactly why some sharks breach, it may be a way to surprise their prey.

The **common thresher** is the biggest of the thresher sharks, sometimes reaching 20 feet long and 1,000 pounds. Though it can be found worldwide, it is most commonly seen in cool waters, both close to shore and in the open ocean.

The **bigeye thresher** reaches 16 feet. Its big eyes measure up to four inches across, and the eyes are taller than they are wide. When bigeye threshers come to the surface at night to hunt, they use their big eyes to see silhouettes of schools of fish in the moonlight.

The **pelagic thresher** is the smallest, usually around 10 feet long. It is the only thresher that is coldblooded and cannot regulate its body temperature. It is the slowest of the threshers and can't tolerate cold waters.

# Basking Sharks

**B**asking sharks amaze anyone who sees them as they swim slowly up and down coastlines all over the world. They are enormous. The second largest shark in the world, basking sharks grow up to 30 feet long and weigh up to 40,000 pounds. But their most distinctive feature is their huge mouth, which stays fully open most of the time. As they swim, small fish and plankton enter their open mouths. The basking shark's tiny teeth separate the water from the fish, which they swallow.

### SINGLE FILE, EVERYONE!

Basking sharks often travel in pairs and sometimes in schools of up to 100 sharks. When they are in groups, they can be seen swimming in a line.

## HEADING SOUTH FOR THE WINTER

Basking sharks are found in the North Atlantic throughout the warmer months of spring, summer, and fall, but no one could figure out where they disappeared to in winter. That is, until 2009, when scientists at the Massachusetts Division of Marine Fisheries decided to solve the mystery. They tagged a group of basking sharks and tracked them using satellite-based technology. When the satellite picked up the sharks' tags off the coast of Brazil, the scientists were surprised. They don't know why basking sharks head south for the winter, but at least they learned where they go.

It's hard to stay afloat when you weigh 40,000 pounds. Other fish have swim bladders, which are gas-filled pockets within their bodies that keep them buoyant, but sharks don't. Instead, sharks have big livers that are filled with oil. The oil is lighter than water, so it gives the shark a bit of a lift. The basking shark's liver is gigantic proportionally— about 25 percent of its total weight—which gives the large shark a helpful boost.

# Megamouth Sharks

On November 15, 1976, a U.S. Navy ship cruising off the coast of the island of Oahu in Hawaii found that its sea anchor (an anchor that drags along in the ocean while the ship is in motion) had picked up something big. When they investigated, they found a large dead fish that no one recognized. They took it to the Waikiki Aquarium, where scientists identified it as a shark—but one that no one had ever seen before. It was named for its large mouth. The rest of the shark was large as well, 14.7 feet long, weighing 1,650 pounds.

The megamouth is different from all other sharks: It is flabby and has loose skin and an oddly shaped mouth lined with silvery membranes. Megamouth sharks are rarely seen, and their discovery was a major one in the world of sharks.

*This megamouth shark was found in Australia.*

## FILTER FEEDING

Megamouth sharks and two of the largest sharks in the world—basking and whale sharks—are big sharks that are not predators of large prey. Instead, they swim with open mouths and have many rows of small teeth. The whale shark has up to 300 teeth, and the megamouth has more than 90. The small teeth are called gill rakers, and they use them to filter the seawater that enters their mouths as they swim. The gill rakers separate the edible portion of each mouthful from the inedible, and the sharks push the edible food toward the back of their mouths. When they have a good batch of food, they swallow it, spit out the water, and start again.

*Basking shark*

*Whale shark*

## RARE FISH

Since the megamouth was first discovered, currently only 54 specimens have been seen, and most of them have been found caught up in fishing nets. They have been found off the coasts of Japan, Taiwan, Hawaii, the Philippines, Indonesia, Australia, Africa, and the west coast of North America. Little is known about the megamouth shark, but scientists continue to study this exciting member of the shark world.

# Goblin Sharks

These deep-sea dwellers have been called the ugliest living sharks, and aliens from outer space. The goblin shark is long, measuring 8 to 12 feet. It is found around the world but is most common near Japan. It has a long, pointed snout, which it uses to dig for shellfish on the ocean floor. Its mouth is filled with needle-sharp teeth that it uses to spear and then tear its prey. In addition to its strange head ornament, it also has a startling way of moving its mouth. When it attacks, it pushes its whole jaw out of its mouth. When it's finished eating, it collapses its jaw back into its mouth.

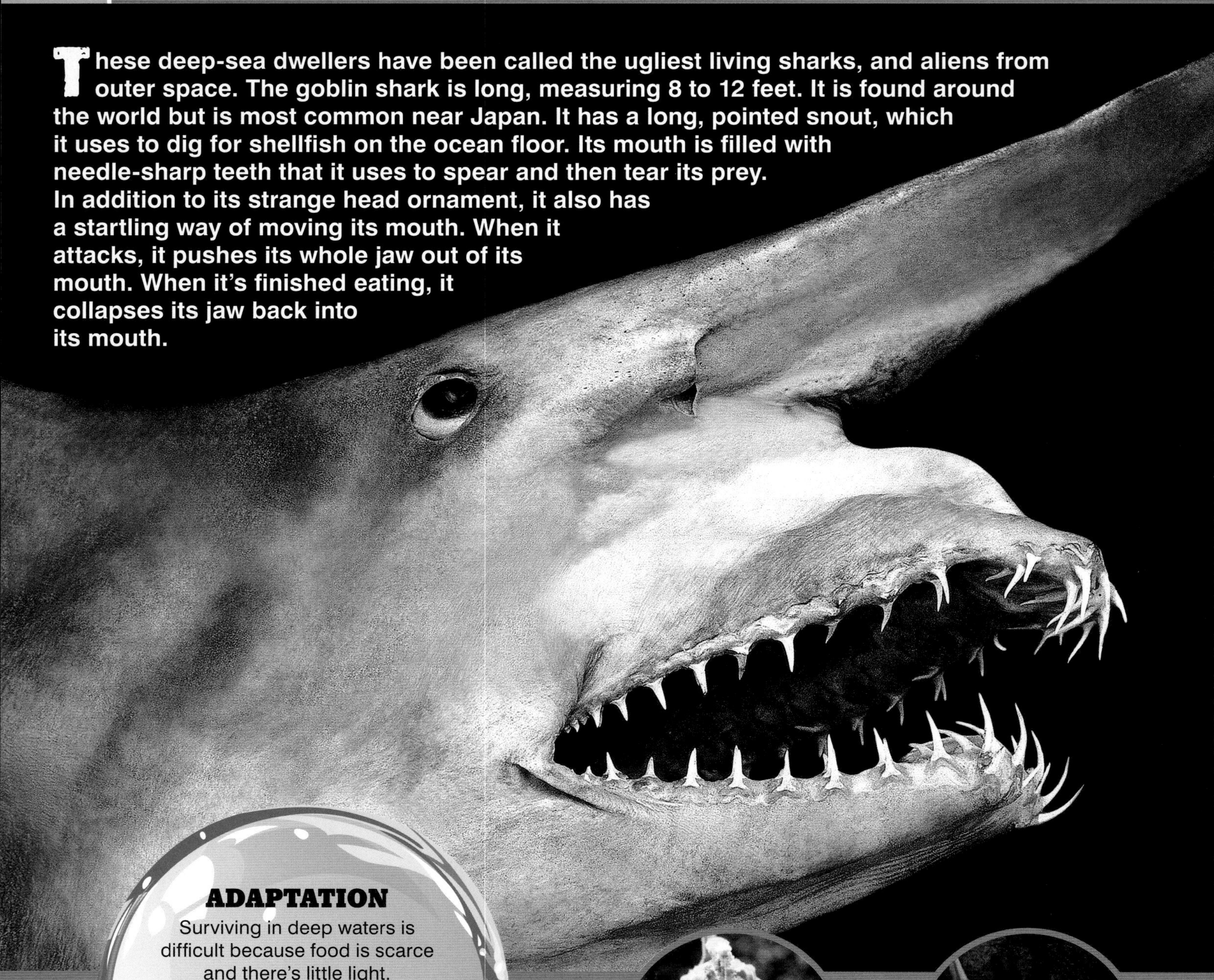

## ADAPTATION
Surviving in deep waters is difficult because food is scarce and there's little light. Deep-sea dwellers, like the ones shown here, often have unusual looks, which scientists believe are the result of adaptations that help them survive.

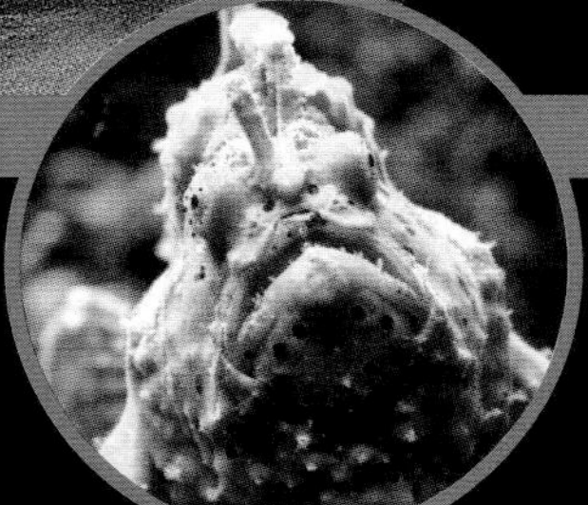

**Yellow angler fish** attract prey with a fleshy attachment near their heads that looks like a fishing pole.

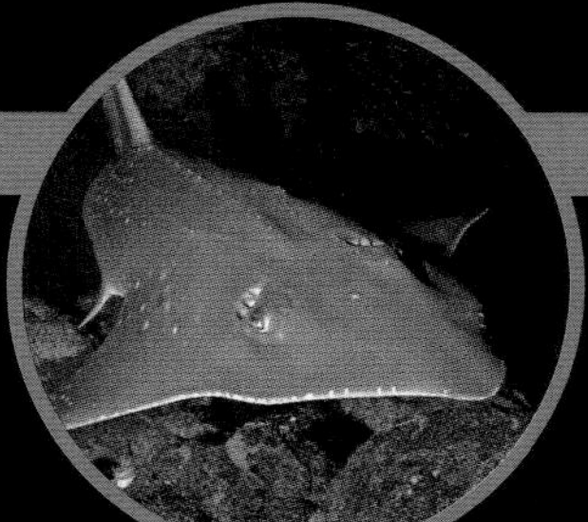

**Shovelnose guitarfish** are rays, which are closely related to sharks; they have a well-developed visual sense.

The goblin shark has a pinkish tone, which makes it unlike any other shark. Why is it pink? The goblin shark's skin is thin and it bruises easily. This leads to broken blood vessels, which can be seen through the thin skin, giving the shark its pink hue.

A goblin shark's jaw collapses back into its mouth after it finishes eating, as shown here.

## GUESS WHAT?

Few goblin sharks have been observed, and no one knows how large the population is. But after an earthquake near China, about 100 dead goblin sharks washed ashore, which makes it seem likely that there is a large population of these strange sharks deep under the ocean waters.

### Seapigs
have tubes on their undersides that—like legs— help them move along the ocean floor.

### Frogfish
are covered with bumps that make them look very unusual.

### Leafy seadragons
look more like plants than fish, which is a good form of camouflage.

# Great White Sharks

Great white sharks are not the biggest or the fastest sharks in the world. But great whites are the sharks that everyone knows and fears the most. This is partly because of sensational stories that portray great whites as vicious, mindless killers. But it is also because great whites are fearsome predators, intelligent and efficient, with streamlined bodies and sharp senses that allow them to hunt with speed, force, and precision. Most sharks have good senses, but great whites are known for their excellent vision and sense of smell.

## SHARK I.D.

Most people will never get close enough to a great white shark to see all its identifying features. Here are some ways to tell if a shark is a great white.

**Teeth**
Several rows of 2- to 2½-inch-high teeth

**Serration**
Great white teeth have sawlike ridges for ripping flesh

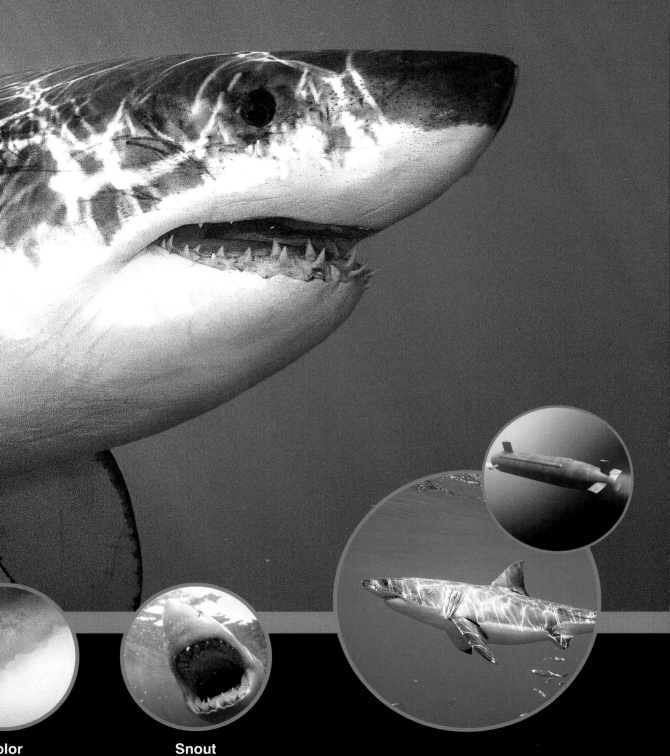

**Color**
Gray on top, white underneath, for camouflage above and below

**Snout**
Great whites have a small, cone-shaped snout.

Both of these are designed to move through the water with great speed. The great white's body shape inspired submarine designs.

# Apex Predators

**M**ost living things are food for other living things. Bigger creatures eat smaller creatures in an arrangement that's known as the food chain. At the bottom of the food chain, plants produce food that is eaten by the smallest organisms, things that are too small for the eye to see. Those organisms are eaten by slightly bigger ones, and so on up to apex predators: creatures that are at the top of the food chain. Apex predators are too big and too powerful to be lunch for anyone else. In the ocean, sharks are apex predators, and great whites are the apex predator of the shark world.

**WORD!**
Apex means "the top" or "highest."

## SUPERIOR SKILLS

The great white shark evolved over millions of years with several features that make it supremely able to survive, such as a superior digestive system, many sharp serrated teeth, and an ability to regulate body temperature that allows it to swim in warmer and cooler waters. The great white's size, speed, powerful jaws, and heightened senses of sight, smell, and electroreception keep it at the top of the food chain.

## BATTLE AT THE TOP OF THE FOOD CHAIN

Great white sharks are not the only apex predators in the ocean; orcas have that status as well. So who wins in a fight between an orca and a great white shark? The great white has sharper senses. But the orca is bigger—the biggest ones are 25 feet long, while the biggest great whites are 20 feet long. In 2003, an orca attacked a great white. It rammed the great white and stunned it, then held it upside down and tore it apart. But there are many times when great whites feed on whales, even orcas.

What makes an apex predator? In some cases, it's a question of size. Orcas and grizzly bears are big enough to stop most animals from preying on them. Some may not be the biggest animals in their environment but have a special feature that makes them powerful, such as the sharp teeth of the piranha, the shock of the electric eel, the strong jaws of the crocodile, and the talons of the bald eagle.

# Breaching

There are few events in nature that come close to the raw power of a great white shark leaping from the ocean, splitting the water, and thrusting its magnificent body into the air. This process is called breaching, and it is mostly seen in great white sharks off the coast of South Africa. In that region, the ocean is fairly shallow, so great white sharks can cruise along the bottom and then thrust upward when they see or sense prey, usually seals or sea lions.

How do sharks make this dramatic maneuver? First, they accelerate as they move up from a depth of about 100 feet. By the time they are under a seal, they are moving at around 20 miles per hour. They hit the seal with the same force as a car crash. Scientists believe that the seal is stunned, unconscious, or possibly dead from the force of the blow before it is eaten by the great white.

## SEAL ISLAND

Great white sharks often visit places where their favorite food is abundant. One example is Seal Island off the coast of Cape Town, South Africa, which is home to large colonies of Cape fur seals. Great whites have a special technique for catching seals. During the season each year when seal pups begin to swim and hunt, a group of great whites circles the island in a "ring of death." When a seal swims off the island in order to find food in the open waters and ventures into this ring, one of the sharks swoops underneath it, breaches, and catches it.

Great white sharks have captured the world's imagination thanks both to their extraordinary feats and to legend and lore. Some individual sharks have been given special nicknames.

**Nicole** migrated more than 12,400 miles from southern Africa to Australia and then back again. Her epic journey is the greatest recorded migration by a great white shark. She was named to honor the actress Nicole Kidman, a staunch advocate for sharks and ocean conservation.

**El Monstruo de Cojimar** was caught off the coast of Cuba in 1945 in what was reported as a long and fierce battle. Everyone from the nearby village of Cojimar came out for the measuring ceremony. The fishermen who caught "El Monstruo" (The Monster) claimed that the shark was over 21 feet long and weighed more than 7,000 pounds. Experts who studied the photographs say the measurements were greatly exaggerated, but the shark continues to be talked about nearly 70 years later.

**Schatzi** (which means "sweetie" or "darling" in German) was named by conservationist and dive captain Jimmy Hall. Hall was diving near a shark cage in Hawaii when a great white swam right up to him. He grabbed his camera equipment and got into the cage. After a while, he left the cage and swam in open waters with the shark. The large great white interacted with him in a completely peaceful way.

**Mary Lee,** a great white named after the mother of a research program's director, was tagged by a research boat in Cape Cod to find out why she disappears every winter. It turns out she goes south, to Florida. Sometimes the group gets a ping that tells them that Mary Lee is swimming by a beach used by people, and they notify officials near that beach to get everyone out of the water.

People have great interest in, and fascination with, sharks. Shark stories, images, and names are popular in books and movies, on T-shirts and kites, in music, on machines and appliances from cars to vacuums, and even as sports team names.

Chompie on Discovery Communications Headquarters in Silver Spring, Maryland

# Mako Sharks

**W**ith their brilliant metallic blue skin and sleek, elegant bodies, mako sharks are among the most beautiful fish in the ocean. They are also one of the fastest. They zip through the water with lightning speed, and in short bursts swim at 44 miles per hour. Makos inhabit temperate and tropical waters all over the world. There are two types of makos: shortfin and longfin. Makos are medium- to large-sized sharks, with males averaging 10 feet long and females averaging 12½ feet.

Makos are built for speed. Their muscles—which are arranged differently from those of other sharks—are like propellers that push their bodies forward. Even their tails have the right proportions to make them move quickly, with maximum forward thrust and minimum drag to slow them down.

### DID YOU KNOW?

Mako sharks are popular characters. The shark that ate the old man's fish in Ernest Hemingway's novel *The Old Man and the Sea* is a mako. So is Chum in the movie *Finding Nemo*.

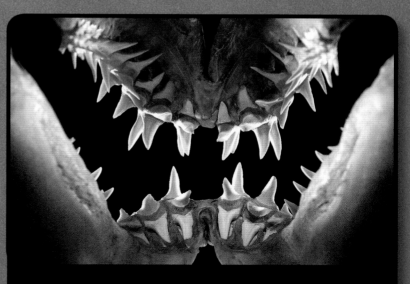

A mako shark's teeth are arranged in a way that makes them visible even when its jaws are closed.

Salmon sharks know what they like: cold water and salmon. They'll also eat squid, sablefish, and herring, but they get their name from their love of salmon. They migrate thousands of miles, but always stay in the North Pacific, where salmon are. Salmon sharks look a lot like great whites, and like their lookalikes, they also have good vision. They are not as big, though, and usually grow 7 to 9 feet long.

## ANDY SAYS

The life span of a salmon shark is estimated at 30 to 40 years, so their population doesn't match the population of the salmon, which live three to four years. It is likely that with low salmon numbers, fewer salmon sharks survive as there is less to eat. Unfortunately, human fishing also likely plays a large role in this.

—*Andy Dehart, Marine Biologist*

## THERMOREGULATION AND THE MIRACLE NET

Salmon sharks are warm-blooded creatures, which means they can regulate their own body temperature. The salmon shark can raise its temperature as much as 60 degrees above the water temperature, which is four times as much as other warm-blooded mackerel sharks. It does this by using a special band of muscle known as a miracle net, which warms its blood as it circulates through its body. Because they can stay warm, salmon sharks can survive in much colder waters than most other sharks, and they can feast on the tasty salmon that live in those colder waters.

## A NEW SPEED RECORD

Salmon sharks are powerful, but the thick shape of their body doesn't seem to be made for speed. They have a stiff swimming style because of their wide bodies, but they can use their tails like propellers. They move their tails back and forth quickly while holding their bodies mostly rigid. They don't maneuver well, but they can move with high speed in a straight line. They are the current title holders as fastest sharks alive: The U.S. Navy clocked salmon sharks swimming at 55 mph, beating the previous winners, shortfin makos.

## WORD!

The "thermo" in thermoregulation means heat or warmth, and "regulation" means adjustment. Thermoregulation allows a creature to raise or lower its body temperature to adjust to its environment.

**S**and tiger sharks—also known as sand sharks, raggedtooth sharks, and grey nurse sharks—have curvy, pointy teeth that make them look like the meanest fish in the ocean. Because of the way their jaws are shaped, their teeth stick out even when their mouths are closed. But sand tigers are not particularly aggressive and are not known to attack people unless they are provoked. They live in warm waters all over the world except the eastern Pacific, where none has been spotted. They tend to stay close to sandy shores, which is how they got their name. Sand tiger sharks are not large, usually around 10 feet long.

## THE SAND TIGER TRICK

Most sharks have to keep swimming to stay afloat, but the sand tiger has a way to hover in the water without swimming and still stay afloat. It raises its head out of the water and gulps big mouthfuls of air, which act like balloons inside and makes it buoyant. When a sand tiger shark wants to sink, it burps out the air.

## TIDBIT

Because of their scary appearance and calm behavior, sand tigers are popular in aquariums. They look fierce but seldom snack on their tank mates.

**P**orbeagle sharks are similar to salmon sharks in several ways: They are good at thermoregulation—changing their body temperature so that they are warmer than the water around them—so they can tolerate cold, even icy, waters. They grow to around 12 feet long, and live near northern coastlines.

## THE FUN SHARKS

Shark researchers are studying porbeagles because they are the first sharks that have been observed seeming to play. People report seeing groups of up to 20 porbeagles playing what looks like tag or football—finball?—by tossing around chunks of debris or seaweed.

Porbeagles have distinctive pointy noses. The cartilage in their noses becomes hard and forms a structure for their cone-shaped snouts.

*Porbeagle snout cartilage*

# The Deadly Quartet

There are nearly 500 different kinds of sharks in the world. Of these, only about a dozen are responsible for more than a few unprovoked bites. When this happens, the injuries are typically not serious or fatal. Of the roughly 500 shark species, there are only four that scientists warn could be of concern to humans because of their feeding style.

## OCEANIC WHITETIP SHARKS

The 10-foot-long, slow-swimming oceanic whitetip sharks cruise near the surface of the ocean, following schools of fish. When a ship runs into trouble and survivors end up in the water, oceanic whitetips take the opportunity to feast. There have been many stories of these sharks biting people from sunken boats, but the most famous is that of the U.S.S. *Indianapolis*, a ship that sank during World War II. More than 800 people survived the shipwreck, but only 321 were alive when rescuers arrived three and a half days later. The loss of so many hundreds of lives is attributed mostly to exposure or dehydration, but many were killed by oceanic whitetip sharks. Documented oceanic whitetip attacks are rare, perhaps because they happen in deep ocean waters where there are few observers and little evidence remains.

Five shark attacks were attributed to oceanic whitetips in less than two weeks in 2010 at Sharm el-Sheikh, a popular Egyptian tourist destination. This is considered to be unprecedented by shark experts. Dozens of sharks in the area were captured and killed. The attacks may have occurred because some dive operators were feeding sharks improperly and because sheep carcasses from a festival had been dumped in the ocean, attracting a large number of sharks.

## BULL SHARKS

Bull sharks are known to have bitten 121 people and have caused 25 deaths—but researchers think that the number should be higher, that many of the bites credited to tigers and great whites were actually from bull sharks. Bull sharks are not very long, but they are heavy and powerful and they swim in shallow water, including freshwater rivers. This means bull sharks come near people more often than other sharks, and that may be one reason why they are a great danger.

In 2001, an eight-year-old boy was bitten by a bull shark near Pensacola, Florida. The shark bit off the boy's arm before the boy's uncle rescued him. As the boy was rushed to a hospital, the uncle wrestled the shark to the shore and pried open its mouth. The arm was retrieved and surgeons successfully reattached it.

### FAST FACT
About 100 people around the world are bitten by sharks each year and on average six people die from shark bites. Some 70 million sharks are killed by people each year.

Shark and human interactions are not uncommon, but shark attacks on humans are rare. Usually, sharks realize that people aren't the prey they are after and they swim away after taking a nip—this is called "bite and release." But even if sharks release their bite quickly, their big teeth can do a lot of damage.

## TIGER SHARKS

Tiger sharks have strong jaws and sharp teeth that are powerful enough to puncture metal. Tiger sharks often swim in shallow water near beaches where there are many surfers and swimmers. It is likely that when tiger sharks do bite humans, it is a case of mistaken identity, with the shark thinking the human is a sea turtle, its favorite food. Tiger sharks have been credited with 157 bites on people, including 27 fatal bites.

In 2003, 13-year-old Bethany Hamilton (above) was surfing off the coast of Kauai, Hawaii. Her left arm was in the water when a tiger shark pulled up alongside her and bit off her arm. Friends tied a tourniquet around her shoulder and helped her to shore. She recovered and still surfs competitively. The movie *Soul Surfer* tells her story.

## GREAT WHITE SHARKS

Almost half of all recorded fatal shark bites have involved great white sharks. There have been 247 documented great white attacks, including 65 fatal ones. Great whites don't really like humans— they usually bite and release. But even a test bite from their huge jaws and teeth is devastating to the human body, and unless the victim can get immediate medical attention, the bite can be fatal.

# Shark Beaches

The oceans are full of sharks, and they share the waters with swimmers in shallow, as well as deep waters. Anyone who spends a lot of time in the ocean has likely come close to sharks at one point or another. The fact is that most sharks aren't interested in people, but there are some beaches around the world that seem to log a higher number of shark bites than others.

**Recife, Brazil,** is a city with a population of nearly five million people located where the Beberibe and Capiberibe rivers meet and flow into the Atlantic Ocean. Bull sharks inhabit both rivers and the ocean, and 14 fatal bites have occurred there.

**New South Wales, Australia.** There have been 877 shark bites in Australia, including 216 fatal ones, since record keeping started in 1792. New South Wales is especially known for shark bites, possibly because it is the most densely populated area along the Australian coast and is a surfing hot spot.

**Second Beach, St. John's Port, South Africa,** has been named "The World's Most Dangerous Beach" because it has been the scene of five shark bites in just over five years, all of them fatal. Although South Africa is famous for an abundance of great white sharks, the bites here were made by bull sharks.

Réunion Island, a French island in the Indian Ocean near Madagascar, has an active surfing community and a booming population of bull and tiger sharks, a dangerous combination. There have been dozens of bites, including three fatal ones.

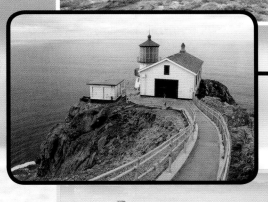

Papua, New Guinea, in the Pacific Ocean, is the world's largest tropical island, and sharks flock to the port city on the island's east side. There is a profitable trade in shark products, including fins. There have been 47 bites to humans there, including 25 fatal ones.

California's Red Triangle. The area between three points—Monterey Bay and Point Reyes on the North California coastline, and the Farallon Islands west of San Francisco—is home to lots of seals and to the great white sharks that feed on them. Bolinas Beach and Stinson Beach are well known great white havens. More than a third of great white bites in the U.S. occur in the Red Triangle.

Broward County, Florida, is the scene of more shark bites than anywhere else in the world, but researchers think that is at least partly because so many people swim and surf in the area and there is a high density of small coastal sharks feeding on bait fish in the same area.

The Oahu and Maui coastlines are home to more than 40 kinds of sharks that swim in the warm waters around the Hawaiian Islands, but tiger sharks are responsible for most of the bites there. Despite the fact that more than seven million people enjoy Hawaii's waters every year, only a handful of bites take place and there has been only one fatality since 2004.

# A Shark Bite Story

In July 1916, a series of shark bites took place on the New Jersey shore that killed four people and injured one. These incidents shocked people and caused a panic across the nation, changing the way people think about sharks.

## WHAT HAPPENED?

In the summer of 1916, there was an extreme heat wave in the eastern U.S. This was before people had air conditioning or backyard pools. Many people flocked to beaches, including the ones along the New Jersey shore. Boat captains reported that sharks of all kinds were especially abundant during that summer, but no one thought much about sharks then.

The first bite occurred on Sunday, July 1. A 25-year-old man took a pre-dinner swim with his dog. When he began screaming, people thought he was calling his dog, but he was actually being bitten by a shark. Though the man was rescued by a lifeguard and a bystander—who said the shark followed them to shore—he ultimately bled to death.

The beaches stayed open; there was no panic at that point. A few days later, on July 6, a 27-year-old bellhop from a local hotel was bitten on the stomach and legs while swimming 130 yards from shore. He, too, bled to death after being pulled from the water.

On July 12, the cases moved to a creek in Matawan, New Jersey. An 11-year-old boy, playing in the water with some friends, was pulled under by an 8-foot-long shark. His friends ran for help and a 25-year-old man jumped in to find the boy—but the shark bit off the rescuer's leg. The boy's body was found 150 miles away. A half hour after the incidents in the stream, another boy was bitten, but he survived.

## THE REACTION

News of the Jersey attacks was on the front pages of newspapers across the nation. There was widespread panic, and beaches up and down both coasts were closed as people organized shark hunts, intending to kill every shark in the ocean. People petitioned the government to protect beaches with nets and to set up government programs to eradicate sharks. Scientists, who had spent little time studying sharks, started new research into how and why sharks bite people—and in the years since have learned a lot about how sharks live.

FINANCIAL EDITION

Evening Ledger

PHILADELPHIA, FRIDAY, JULY 7, 1916.

MAN-EATING SHARK OF VARIETY WHICH INFESTS ATLANTIC

QUICK NEWS

Map showing locations: New York City, Coney Isl., Raritan Bay, Matawan July 12, Asbury Park, Spring Lake July 6, Philadelphia, Beach Haven July 1, Atlantic City, Atlantic Ocean. …more, 1916

## WHICH SHARK WAS RESPONSIBLE?

Since 1916, scientists have debated this question. Some medium-sized sharks were caught in the area, including a blue shark and a sandbar shark, but scientists said that they were probably too small to have done the damage. A young great white shark was found a few days later, and it was dubbed "the Jersey Man-Eater," but scientists still debate whether a single young shark was responsible for the attacks, and why they happened. Given that a few of the bites took place up a brackish creek, many scientists believe a bull shark was the culprit for the Matawan Creek case.

*Great white shark*

*Bull shark*

### DID YOU KNOW?

These shark attacks are credited with inspiring the book *Jaws*, written by Peter Benchley, and the Stephen Spielberg movie based on it.

After repeated reports on what were then considered shark attacks on servicemen during World War II, the Navy decided that it needed to collect information about attacks so that it could protect its people. The U.S. International Shark Attack File is now housed at the Florida Museum of Natural History at the University of Florida and contains detailed reports of more than 5,000 shark bites from the 1500s to today. (The earlier attacks are based on unconfirmed information that survived from centuries ago.) While the individual shark attack reports are available only to serious researchers, there is a great deal of information available on the ISAF website, flmnh.ufl.edu/fish/sharks/isaf/isaf.htm.

## NUMBER OF SHARK BITES PER YEAR, WORLDWIDE

When a shark bite occurs it is generally referred to as a shark attack and people often panic and assume that shark attacks are on the rise. The number of shark bites is actually fairly steady and lower than people assume.

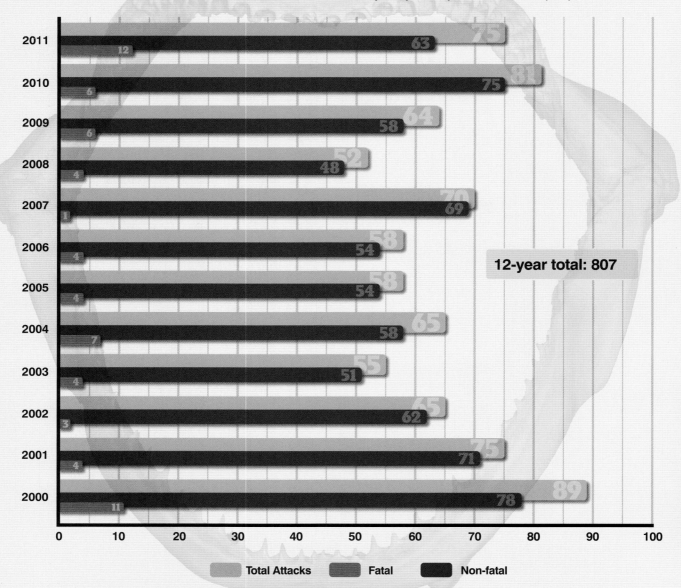

12-year total: 807

Legend: Total Attacks — Fatal — Non-fatal

| Year | Total Attacks | Non-fatal | Fatal |
|------|---------------|-----------|-------|
| 2011 | 75 | 63 | 12 |
| 2010 | 81 | 75 | 6 |
| 2009 | 64 | 58 | 6 |
| 2008 | 52 | 48 | 4 |
| 2007 | 70 | 69 | 1 |
| 2006 | 58 | 54 | 4 |
| 2005 | 58 | 54 | 4 |
| 2004 | 65 | 58 | 7 |
| 2003 | 55 | 51 | 4 |
| 2002 | 65 | 62 | 3 |
| 2001 | 75 | 71 | 4 |
| 2000 | 89 | 78 | 11 |

**Triggers** Sharks don't bite people because they are trying to kill them but rather because they are checking to see if they are good food to eat. Some behaviors that attract a curious shark are splashing in the water and sharp contrasts in color, which can be caused by shiny jewelry, brightly colored clothing, or uneven tan lines.

## FAST FACT

Why do sharks bite surfers? From underwater, surfboards resemble sea lions, seals, or sea turtles, favorite food items for some shark species.

There were 2,463 confirmed unprovoked shark bites around the world between 1588 and 2011. Of these, 471 were fatal.

The United States had the highest number of incidents, with 980 total overall between 1588 and 2011, but in that same period there were 488 attacks in Australia, and 144 of them resulted in death.

In 2011, the ISAF investigated 125 reported shark attacks. Of these, 75 were confirmed to be unprovoked attacks. There were 12 fatal attacks.

The average number of people who get killed by a shark in the United States is 1 per year; more than 3,300 people on average die from drowning each year in the U.S.

More than 80 percent of people who are bitten by sharks live to tell the tale. Here are just a few stories from people who survived shark attacks.

## COOKIECUTTER ATTACK

Cookiecutter sharks are known for their unique approach to eating. They don't try to devour their prey—they use their many teeth to take a bite, leaving a round cookie-shaped scar. Because they don't need to overpower and kill their prey, cookiecutters can feast on bites from animals many times their size, including killer whales and great white sharks. They are not known for attacking people.

But on the evening of March 16, 2009, while marathon swimmer Mike Spalding was training near Hawaii, he received several painful bites that were identified as being consistent with those of a cookiecutter shark. It was the first report of a cookiecutter attack on a human being. Spalding says, "I felt a sharp prick just to the left of my sternum. It was excruciating and I gave a yelp. As soon as that happened I knew I had to get out of the water and the swim was over…. As I was about to push onto the kayak I felt a hit on my left calf. I ran my finger down my leg and felt a 2½- by ¾-inch hole where I had been hit." The bite was painful, but not life threatening. He is still training for marathons by swimming in the ocean.

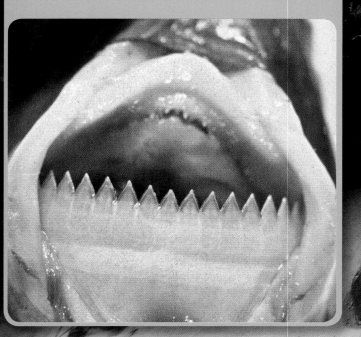

## EXPERT VICTIM

Experts know that sharks are unpredictable and that attacks can happen to anyone at any time. But still, the attack on Dr. Erich Ritter, a Discovery Channel shark expert, was shocking. It happened in March 2002, while he was filming a segment about how most sharks ignore humans in clear water. The water was not very clear that day—in fact, it was quite murky. So, in a painful way, he proved his point—murky waters trigger some shark attacks. A 350-pound bull shark grabbed Dr. Ritter's leg and bit a huge chunk out of it. It was a severe bite, but Dr. Ritter recovered from the attack and he continues his work on the body language of sharks. He also trains divers in how to be safe around sharks.

# SHARK VS. SURFER

California surfer Eric Tarantino was bitten by a shark just minutes after he entered the water off Monterey Bay. He saw the shark coming, but wasn't able to get out of the way fast enough. He was lucky—he survived the attack. By inspecting the 19-inch gashes and tooth marks on Tarantino's surfboard, experts determined the attacker was a large great white shark. Surfers are among the most common shark-attack victims.

**Tarantino says that the experience of having his arm in the shark's mouth was like being pulled by a truck.**

# CAGE ATTACK

People who go cage-diving want to see sharks up close, but they don't want to be eaten, and the 5- by 7-foot steel cages used in cage-diving adventures are built to withstand bites from great white sharks. But sometimes things don't go as planned. Jerry Lohman and Pieter Boshoff were on a cage-diving adventure when a great white shark charged their cage. The shark was chasing chum, or bait, thrown into the water from the boat on the surface to attract sharks. Electrical impulses given off by the metal of the cage may also have been sensed by the shark's ampullae of Lorenzini. The shark broke through the cage's bars and got stuck. The two men inside were eye to eye with the great white shark, just inches from the shark's jaw as it thrashed around. The men lay on their backs on the bottom of the cage to avoid being bitten as the shark got closer and closer. Then they became disconnected from their air supply. The terrified men were able to slip out of the cage and swim back to the boat. Boshoff will never go cage-diving again. "I'll never forget that eye," he says.

**SAWSHARKS**
*Pristiophoridae*
African Dwarf Sawshark
Bahamas Sawshark
Dwarf Sawshark
Eastern Sawshark
Japanese Sawshark
Longnose Sawshark
Philippine Sawshark
Shortnose Sawshark
Sixgill Sawshark
Tropical Sawshark

# Sawsharks

These odd-looking sharks have two sets of teeth. The first runs along the sides of their long, flat, broad snouts, called rostrums. This makes the rostrum an effective tool for raking the ocean floor to find food and tearing it up into bite-sized pieces. The snout has barbels with sensory organs attached, which may help the sawshark identify good things to eat on the ocean floor. The teeth along the edges of the snout alternate: long-short-long-short. Sawsharks also have small mouths on the undersides of their snouts, with many rows of teeth inside that they use to grab pieces of food.

## Highlights

### ORDER

Sawsharks
*Pristiophoriformes*

### NAME

Sawsharks are named for their saw-shaped snouts.

### SPECIES

There are 10 sawsharks in one family.

### SIZE

Most sawsharks are about 4 feet long, but the dwarf, tropical, and Bahamas sawsharks are about 2 feet long.

### HABITAT

Most live in the western Pacific or the Indian Ocean between South Africa and Australia. A few live in the Bahamas and in the northwestern and southeastern Atlantic.

# Long Snout, Small Mouth

Sawsharks have developed a technique for finding and killing their prey. They swim to the ocean floor, then use their special sensory organs—the ampullae of Lorenzini and the barbels hanging from their snouts—to help them sense where crustaceans, squid, and small fish are hiding in the sand. When they find something good to eat, they use their sawlike snout to stun, kill, and rip it apart.

*Sawfish*

Sawsharks and sawfish look similar and are closely related. But sawfish teeth don't alternate between long and short as sawshark teeth do. And sawfish teeth are rooted; sawshark teeth have no roots, so they fall out easily and are replaced.

Sawshark pups are born from eggs that hatch within their mother's stomach. Until the pups are born, the teeth on their snouts are folded flat. The teeth pop out after they are born.

Sawsharks have small mouths on the undersides of their heads. The teeth in their mouths are small and more flat than pointed. These teeth are used for crushing the pieces that the sharp teeth on the snouts have torn apart.

# Recently Discovered Sharks

As people discover new ways to travel deeper in the ocean and new technologies to study animals, many more discoveries may be made. Scientists undertake research missions to study the sea creatures that they find and take photos, videos, and detailed notes. In some years, as many as a dozen new species may be described and made official when they are published in scientific journals.

## RECENT DISCOVERIES

John McCosker, chairman of aquatic biology at the California Academy of Sciences, was on a research mission near the Galapagos Islands when he looked out the window of his submersible vessel and saw a shark that looked different from any he had seen before. He turned the vehicle around and chased the small shark, finally scooping it and several others from the ocean. The dark brown shark had spots distributed randomly over its body, which was unusual. This made the scientists think it was a new species.

When they got back to shore, they wrote a detailed description of the specimen, pointing out the unusual color and pattern, its sharp teeth, its body size, how its fins were positioned, and where they had found it. They waited for DNA testing, to make sure it had not already been described. It took many years for the find to become official. Their description was published in the March 5, 2012 edition of the journal *Zootaxa* and now the Galapagos catshark, also called *Bythaelurus giddingsi*, is an official new shark.

## TIDBIT

New techniques for exploring the depths of the ocean, such as better submersibles (vehicles for descending into the deep) and new ways of analyzing DNA, have led to many official new shark species.

ATLANTIS
WOODS HOLE

New shark species are discovered all the time. Thirty years ago, only about 250 sharks were known and described in scientific journals. Today, there are almost 500 known species of sharks and there may be many more in the world's oceans waiting to be found.

## WHAT'S NEW IN THE SHARK WORLD?

Some new sharks are just slight variations of existing species, such as a new hammerhead shark species that was initially thought to be the scalloped hammerhead. Recent advances in genetics and DNA testing have helped scientists confirm that this is actually a new species. Other new species have interesting new features, such as the taillight shark which emits glowing blue bubbles from a sac on its abdomen, and a new sawshark that has a swordlike nose.

## ANDY SAYS

Sharks are fascinating animals! At a time when sharks need further research to ensure their survival, and with the advances in DNA testing for new species, now is a perfect time to get into a career working with these amazing animals. There are many like myself working with sharks currently, but we need the next generation interested in these animals to pursue science so they can carry on the efforts to better understand sharks and to help protect them.

—Andy Dehart, Marine Biologist

There are many good ways to get close to sharks and learn more, including visiting them in an aquarium, watching television shows and series such as Discovery Channel's "Shark Week," reading informative and exciting books like this one, and joining organizations dedicated to helping sharks. Several of these are listed below. All the aquariums listed are good places to see sharks; a few of the more notable shark inhabitants are identified, but visitors will see many more. And the organizations all have diverse and varied programs and initiatives.

## AQUARIUMS

### CALIFORNIA

**Aquarium of the Bay**
The Embarcadero
at Beach Street, Pier 39
San Francisco, CA 94133
(415) 623-5300
aquariumofthebay.org
*Angelsharks and sevengill sharks*

**Aquarium of the Pacific**
100 Aquarium Way
Long Beach, CA 90802
(562) 590-3100
aquariumofpacific.org
*Sand tiger sharks*

**Birch Aquarium**
2300 Expedition Way
La Jolla, CA 92037
(858) 534-4109
aquarium.ucsd.edu
*Leopard, nurse, blacktip and whitetip reef sharks*

**Monterey Bay Aquarium**
886 Cannery Row
Monterey, CA 93940
(831) 648-4800
montereybayaquarium.org
*Zebra, whitetip reef, and scalloped hammerhead sharks*

**SeaWorld San Diego**
500 SeaWorld Drive
San Diego, CA 92109
(619)222-6363
seaworld.org
*Sand tiger and reef sharks*

**Steinhart Aquarium at California Academy of Sciences**
55 Music Concourse Drive
San Francisco, CA 94118
(415) 379-5152
calacademy.org/academy/exhibits/aquarium
*Blacktip reef and pajama sharks*

### COLORADO

**Landry's Downtown Aquarium**
700 Water Street
Denver, CO 80211
(303) 561-4450
downtownaquarium.com
*Sand tiger, sandbar, and zebra sharks*

### CONNECTICUT

**Mystic Aquarium**
55 CooganBoulevard
Mystic, CT 06355
(860) 572-5955
mysticaquarium.org
*Bamboo, dogfish, and bonnethead sharks*

### FLORIDA

**The Florida Aquarium**
701 Channelside Drive
Tampa, FL 33602
(813) 273-4000
flaquarium.org
*Sand tiger and reef sharks*

**SeaWorld Orlando**
7007 SeaWorld Drive
Orlando, FL 32821
(407) 351-3600
seaworld.org
*Sand tiger and reef sharks*

### GEORGIA

**Georgia Aquarium**
225 Baker Street Northwest
Atlanta, GA 30313
(404) 581-4000
georgiaaquarium.org
*Whale sharks (currently the only ones in an aquarium in the United States)*

### ILLINOIS

**John G. Shedd Aquarium**
1200 South Lake Shore Drive
Chicago, IL 60605
(312) 939-2438
Sheddaquarium.org
*Zebra and blacktip sharks*

### KENTUCKY

**Newport Aquarium**
One Aquarium Way
Newport, KY 41071
(859) 261-7444
newportaquarium.com
*Whitetip and blacktip reef sharks, sand tiger, and zebra sharks*

### LOUISIANA

**Audubon Aquarium of the Americas**
One Canal Street
New Orleans, LA 70130
(504) 565-3033
auduboninstitute.org
*Hammerheads, reef sharks, and sand tiger sharks*

### MARYLAND

**National Aquarium**
501 East Pratt Street, Pier 3
Baltimore, MD 21202
(410) 576-3800
aqua.org
*Chain catsharks, horn sharks, and leopard sharks*

### MASSACHUSETTS

**New England Aquarium**
Central Wharf
Boston, MA 02110
(617) 973-5200
neaq.org
*Coral catsharks, epaulette, and nurse sharks*

### NEBRASKA

**Omaha's Henry Doorly Zoo & Aquarium**
3701 South 10th Street
Omaha, NE 68107
(402) 738-8401
omahazoo.com
*Sand tiger and zebra sharks*

### NEW JERSEY

**Adventure Aquarium**
One Riverside Drive
Camden, NJ 08103
(856) 365-3300
adventureaquarium.com
*Great hammerhead (currently the only one in an aquarium in the United States)*

### NEW YORK

**New York Aquarium**
Surf Avenue at West 8th Street
Brooklyn, NY 11224
(718) 265-3400
nyaquarium.com
*New shark tank opening soon*

### NORTH CAROLINA

**North Carolina Aquarium at Fort Fisher**
900 Loggerhead Road
Kure Beach, NC 28449
(910) 458-8257
ncaquariums.com
*Bamboo and sand tiger sharks*

### OHIO

**Columbus Zoo and Aquarium**
4850 West Powell Road
Powell, OH 43065
(614) 645-3400
columbuszoo.org/
*Bonnethead shark*

## OREGON

**Oregon Coast Aquarium**
2820 Southeast Ferry Slip
Road
Newport, OR 97365
(541) 867-3474
aquarium.org
*Horn sharks and filetail catsharks*

## PENNSYLVANIA

**Pittsburgh Zoo & PPG Aquarium**
One Wild Place
Pittsburgh, PA 15206
(412) 665-3640
pittsburghzoo.com
*Blacktip reef and zebra sharks*

## SOUTH CAROLINA

**Ripley's Aquarium**
1110 Celebrity Circle
Myrtle Beach, SC 29577
(843) 916-0888
ripleysaquarium.com
*Sand tiger, sandbar, and nurse sharks*

## TENNESSEE

**Ripley's Aquarium of the Smokies**
88 River Road
Gatlinburg, TN 37788
(865) 430-8808
ripleysaquarium
ofthesmokies.com
*Sand tiger and nurse sharks*

**Tennessee Aquarium**
One Broad Street
Chattanooga, TN 37401
(800) 262-0695
tnaqua.org
*Epaulette, sand tiger, and sandbar sharks*

## TEXAS

**Houston Aquarium, Inc.**
410 Bagby Street
Houston, TX 77002
(713) 315-5000
downtownaquarium.com
*Nurse and baby bamboo sharks*

**SeaWorld San Antonio**
10500 SeaWorld Drive
San Antonio, TX 78251
(210) 523-3000
seaworld.org
*Sand tiger and reef sharks*

## VIRGINIA

**Virginia Aquarium and Marine Science Center**
717 General Booth Blvd
Virginia Beach, VA 23451
(757) 385-7777
virginiaaquarium.com
*Sand tiger sharks*

## WASHINGTON

**Seattle Aquarium**
1483 Alaskan Way, Pier 59
Seattle, WA 98101
(206) 386-4300
seattleaquarium.org
*Sixgill sharks*

## CANADA

**Vancouver Aquarium Marine Science Center**
845 Avison Way
Vancouver, BC V6G 3E2
(604) 659-3474
vanaqua.org
*Wobbegong, zebra, and dogfish sharks*

## COMNG SOON

**Ripley's Aquarium of Canada**
Toronto, Ontario
Director of Husbandry:
Andy Dehart

## ORGANIZATIONS

**International Union for Conservation of Nature (IUCN)**
*iucn.org*
Learn more about
biodiversity and why it is
important to maintain the
populations of sharks and
other creatures.
The IUCN Red List
(iucnredlist.org) is the
generally accepted source
for the status of wild species;
it assesses the extinction risk
of sharks and other creatures.
Their designations are
Vulnerable, Endangered, and
Critically Endangered (the
highest risk of extinction).

**Oceana**
*oceana.org*
Learn about conservation
and protection of marine
animals like sharks and sea
turtles.

**Shark Savers**
*sharksavers.org*
Learn about sharks and
manta rays, conservation,
and protection.

**The Shark Trust**
*sharktrust.org*
Learn about shark biology,
skates and rays, and
conservation.

**Shark Whisperer**
*sharkwhisperer.org*
Founded in 2011 by then
15-year-old Sara Brenes,
also called "The Shark
Whisperer," to promote the
conservation of sharks.
Started Shark Advocacy
Week in her school.  More
information is available on
the website.

## BOOKS

***Sharks of the World***
*Written by leading shark
authorities Leonardo
Compagno and Sarah Fowler,
with illustrations by wildlife
artist Marc Dando*

*Sharks of the World* is
considered the definitive
field guide to sharks, and it
provides detailed information
about more than 440 known
shark species. *Sharkopedia*
identifies a greater number
of shark species, because
more new sharks have been
discovered since the latest
edition of *Sharks of the World*
was published in 2005.

***The Big Book of Sharks***
**by the Discovery Channel**

*The Big Book of Sharks*
celebrates the 25th
anniversary of Discovery
Channel's "Shark Week,"
capturing all the excitement
that keeps people glued to
their television sets every
summer.

"Shark Week" has been
around for 26 years—longer
than anything Discovery has
aired since its inception in
1985. And over those years,
everyone has grown to love
"Shark Week" for one reason
or another. Some check it
out year after year to learn
the latest in shark behavior,
but most are glued to their
TVs to see every slo-mo
shark-chomping second.
"Shark Week" has become
so ingrained with pop
culture that it's rare to see a
celebrity mention Discovery
without mentioning "Shark
Week," and celebrities
clamor to host this fin-tastic
midsummer programming.
Sharks are synonymous with
Discovery, and the fact of
the matter is that the shark
itself has become our most
notable and long-standing
celebrity. Everyone waits for
those hot summer months
to see the shark take center
stage. And to build on the
excitement, *Sharkopedia*
delivers on bringing fans
fascinating information
about these ultimate
predators. Take a deeper
dive at sharkweek.com.

## PHOTO CREDITS

### FRONT COVER
©Discovery Channel/
Chris Fallows
**Back cover:** ©Deano Cook

**p. 1:** ©Darryl Brooks/
Shutterstock.com **pp. 2-3:**
©Deano Cook **pp. 4-5:**
©Deano Cook **p. 6:** ©Stuart
Cove's Dive Bahama

### SHARK ANATOMY
**pp. 8-9:** Background:
©ptashka/Shutterstock.com
Clockwise from top left:
©solarseven/Shutterstock.
com; ©Greg Amptman's
Undersea Discoveries/
Shutterstock.com; ©Velora/
Shutterstock.com; ©Gary
Bell/OceanwideImages,com;
©Chris & Monique Fallows/
Oceanwidelmages.
com; ©Krzysztof Wictor/
Shutterstock.com; ©A
Cotton Photo/Shutterstock.
com; ©Andrea Izzotti/
Shutterstock.com **pp. 10-11:**
©Andrea Izzotti/Shutterstock.
com **pp. 12-13:** Background:
©Discovery Channel/
Getty Images; Bottom left:
©NaturePL/SuperStock; Top:
©Hemera Technologies/
Photos.com; Bottom right:
©FAUP/Shutterstock.
com **pp. 14-15:** Background:
©NaturePL/SuperStock **p. 14:**
Top left: ©Narchuk/
Shutterstock.com; Bottom left:
©Gary Bell/OceanwideImages.
com **p. 15:** Top left: ©aquapix/
Shutterstock.com; Top right:
©Visual & Written/SuperStock;
Bottom left: ©Greg Amptman's
Undersea Discoveries/
Shutterstock.com; Bottom
right: ©cdelacy/Shutterstock.
com **pp. 16-17:** Background:
©vladoskan/Shutterstock.
com; Far left: ©Shane Gross/
Shutterstock.com; Bottom
center: ©Natursports/
Shutterstock.com; Bottom
right: ©SSSCCC/Shutterstock.
com; Far right, top to
bottom: ©A Cotton Photo/
Shutterstock.com; ©Andy
Murch/OceanwideImages.
com; ©NaturePL/SuperStock;
©Andy Dehart **pp. 18-19:**
Background: ©Discovery
Channel/Chris Fallows;
Center left: ©Kipling Brock/
Shutterstock.com; Center
right: ©Michael Bogner/
Shutterstock.com; Top right:

©Zebra0209/Shutterstock.
com; Bottom right: ©Greg
Amptman's Undersea
Discoveries/Shutterstock.com

### SHARK ORDERS
**pp. 20-21:** Background:
©Hunor Focze/Shutterstock.
com; Top left: ©Miro Vrlik
Photography/Shutterstock.
com ; Bottom left: ©Greg
Amptman's Undersea
Discoveries/Shutterstock.com;
Far right, top to bottom: ©Smit/
Shutterstock.com; ©Vitaly
Korovin/Shutterstock.com;
©Andrea Izzotti/Shutterstock.
com; ©SWFSC/NOAA Fishery
Service; ©kbrowne41/
Shutterstock.com; ©SWFSC/
NOAA Fishery Service; ©Mark
Conlin/NOAA.gov **p. 22:**
Background: ©Willyam
Bradberry/Shutterstock.com
Clockwise from top left: ©Chris
Moncrieff/Dreamstime.com;
Minden Pictures/©SuperStock;
©Discovery Channel/Caterina
Gennaro; ©Rudie Kuiter/
OceanwideImages.com;
©Chad King/SIMoN NOAA;
©Boris Pamkov/Shutterstock.
com **p. 23:** Clockwise from top
left: ©NaturePL/SuperStock;
©Mark Doherty/Shutterstock.
com; ©Greg Amptman's
Undersea Discoveries/
Shutterstock.com; ©Dr. John
Randall, Hawaii; ©Christophe
Testi/Dreamstime.com

### ANGELSHARKS
**pp. 24-25:** ©NaturePL/
Superstock **pp. 26-27:**
Background: ©Nneirda/
Shutterstock.com **p. 26:** ©Phil
Colla/SeaPics.com **p. 27:** Left:
©Stephen Nash/Shutterstock.
com; Right: ©Stephen Wong;
Bottom row, left to right: ©Gary
Bell/OceanwideImages.com;
©Ryo Sato/Creative Commons
Attribution-Share Alike 2.0
Generic license; ©Chris
Moncrieff/Dreamstime.com;
©Bill Boyd/OceanwideImages.
com; ©grabart/Shutterstock.
com

### HABITATS
**pp. 28-29:** Background
and lower left: ©Yuri Arcus/
Shutterstock.com **p. 28:**
Clockwise from top left:
©Ian Scott/Shutterstock.
com; ©Matthew D. Potenski;
©aslysun/Shutterstock.
com; ©Sung Sook/GNU Free
Documentation License **p. 29:**

Background: ©Rich Carey/
Shutterstock.com; Top to
bottom: ©Terry Goss/GNU
Free Documentation License;
©NaturePL/SuperStock;
©FAUP/Shutterstock.
com **pp. 30-31:** Background:
©Vkad61/Shutterstock.
com **p. 31:** ©Michael
Rothschild/Shutterstock.com

### CARPETSHARKS
**pp. 32-33:** ©Ian Scott/
Shutterstock.com **pp. 34-
35:** Background: ©David
Fleetham/Oceanwideimages.
com; Bottom row, left
to right: ©Andy Murch/
oceanwideimages.com; ©Andy
Murch/OceanwideImages.
com; ©FLPA/Superstock;
©Brandelet/Shutterstock.com;
©Nomad/Superstock **p. 34:**
Top: ©Dave Fleetham/Pacific
Stock/Design Pics/Superstock;
Bottom: ©Pufferfishy/
Dreamstime.com **p. 37:**
©Gary Bell/Oceanwideimages.
com **pp. 36-37:** Background:
©Beth Swanson/Shutterstock.
com **p. 36:** Top: ©Greg
Amptman's Undersea
Discoveries/Shutterstock.
com; Bottom: ©holbox/
Shutterstock.com **p. 37:** Top:
©Sergey Dobrov/Shutterstock.
com; Bottom: ©Shane Gross/
Shutterstock.com **pp. 38-
39:** Background: ©Gary Bell/
Oceanwideimages.com **p. 38:**
Top: ©NHPA/SuperStock;
Bottom left: ©Andy Murch/
Oceanwideimages.com;
Bottom right: ©Joel Bauchat
Grant/Shutterstock.com **p. 39:**
Top: ©Thorken/Dreamstime.
com; Bottom: ©Rudie
Kuiter/Oceanwideimages.
com **pp. 40-41:** Background:
©Joanne Weston/
Shutterstock.com; Top right:
©National Geographic/
SuperStock; Bottom right:
©Fionaayerst/Dreamstime.
com

### SENSES
**p. 42:** Left: ©Greg Amptman's
Undersea Discoveries/
Shutterstock.com; Right:
©Chris & Monique Fallows/
Oceanwideimages.
com **p. 43:** Top to bottom:
©Jim Agronick/Shutterstock.
com; ©mp cz/Shutterstock.
com; ©NOAA Fisheries
Service; ©mindaugas13/
istockphoto.com; Discovery
Channel **pp. 44-45:**

Background: ©cbpix/
Shutterstock.com **p. 44:**
Top left: Andy Murch/
OceanwideImages.com;
Bottom left: ©Greg Amptman's
Undersea Discoveries /
Shutterstock.com; Bottom
right: ©NOAA Fisheries
Service **p. 45:** Top left:
©JLFCapture /istockphoto.
com; Right, top to bottom:
©MP cz/Shutterstock.com;
©Natursports/Shutterstock.
com; ©NatalieJean/
Shutterstock.com; ©NOAA
Fisheries Service **pp. 46-47:**
Background: ©Jim Agronick/
Shutterstock.com; Left:
©Laurajel/Dreamstime.com;
Bottom right: ©Natursports/
Shutterstock.com; Top
right: ©Greg Amptman's
Undersea Discoveries/
Shutterstock,com **pp. 48-49:**
Background: ©Albert kok/
GNU Free Documentation
License; Right: ©Brandelest/
Shutterstock.com

### FRILLED SHARKS
### AND COWSHARKS
**pp. 50-51:** ©Tobias
Friedrich/F1 ONLINE/
SuperStock **pp. 52-53:**
Background: ©Getty Images
News/Getty Images **p. 52:**
Bottom: © Getty Images News/
Getty Images **p. 53:** Top:
©Discovery Channel/Caterina
Gennaro; Bottom: ©Marty
Snyderman

### EXTINCT SPECIES
**pp. 54-55:** Background:
©Lunamarina/Dreamstime.
com; Top to bottom
©FunkMonk/GNU Free
Documentation License;
©Jon Borokowski; ©Dmitry
Bogdanov/GNU Free
Documentation License;
©Haplochrums/GNU Free
Documentation License;
©Baxternator/istockphoto.
com **p. 56:** ©Lehakok/
Dreamstime.com **p. 57:** Top
left: ©Dmitry Bogdanov/GNU
Free Documentation License;
Top right: ©Ironrodart/
Dreamstime.com; Bottom:
©Coreyford/Dreamstime.com

### BRAMBLE,
### ROUGHSHARKS,
### LANTERN SHARKS, AND
### OTHER DOGFISH SHARKS
**pp. 58-59:** ©Thediver123/
Dreanstune.com **pp. 60-
61:** Background: ©Boris

# Photo Credits

Snyderman **p. 127**: ©Gary Neil Corbett/SuperStock

**SHARK RESEARCH**
**pp. 128-129**: Background: ©BlueGreen Pictures/SuperStock **p. 128**: ©Boris Pamikov **p. 130-131**: Background: ©Scubazoo/Science Faction/SuperStock; Left, #1, 3, 4, 5: ©Minden Pictures/SuperStock; #2: ©Scubazoo/Science Faction/SuperStock **p. 131**: Top: ©Matthew D. Potenski; Bottom: ©Stuart Cove's Dive Bahama

**WEASEL SHARKS**
**pp. 132-133**: Background: ©Thomas Eder/Shutterstock.com; Shark: ©Dr. John Randall, Hawaii **pp. 134-135**: Background: ©NataliSund/Shutterstock.com **p. 134**: Left: ©Spotty 11222; Right: ©Joe Quinn/Shutterstock.com **p. 135**: Top left: ©Robynrg/Shutterstock.com; Top right: ©Dr. John Randall, Hawaii; Filmstrip ©Virginie Abrial—PURE Diving (Professional Underwater Rebreather Explorers, info@purediving.com)

**SHARK CONSERVATION**
**pp. 136-137**: Backgound: ©Ethan Daniels/Shutterstock. **p. 136**: Top to bottom: ©Eliro/Shutterstock.com; ©NOAA; ©Biosphoto/SuperStock; ©Jose115/Shutterstock.com **p. 137**: ©Chris & Monique Fallows/OceanwideImages.com **pp. 138-139**: ©Ethan Daniels/Shutterstock.com

**HORN SHARKS AND BULLHEAD SHARKS**
**pp. 140-141**: ©Andy Murch/OceanwideImages.com **pp. 142-143**: Background: ©David Fleetham/OceanwideImages.com **p. 143**: Top: ©Biosphoto/SuperStock; Bottom: ©Minden Pictures/SuperStock

**RECORD BREAKERS**
**pp. 144-145**: Background: ©Sakala/Shutterstock.com **p. 144**: Top to bottom: ©Ethan Daniels/Shutterstock.com; ©cdelacy/Shutterstock.com; ©Greg Amptman's Undersea Discoveries/Shutterstock.com **pp. 146-**

**147**: Background: ©irabel8/Shutterstock.com **p. 146**: Top to bottom: ©Andy Dehart; ©Bryan Toro/istockphoto.com; ©Sergey Dubrov /Shutterstock.com **p. 147**: Top to bottom: ©Mark Conlin VWPics; ©Matt Howry/GNU Free Documentation License; ©Steve Bloom Images/SuperStock

**MACKEREL SHARKS**
**pp. 148-149**: ©Gary Bell/OceanwideImages.com **pp. 150-151**: Background: ©nicolas.voisin44/Shutterstock.com **p. 151**: Top to bottom: ©nicolas.voisin44/Shutterstock.com; ©Beth Swanson/Shutterstock.com; ©NOAA Fisheries Service; ©Dray van Beeck/Shutterstock.com **pp. 152-153**: Background: ©Andy Murch/OceanwideImages.com **p. 152**: ©Wayne Davis/OceanAerials.com **p. 153**: Left: ©Greg Skomal/NOAA Fisheries Service; Right: ©Krzysztof Odziomek/Shutterstock.com **pp. 154-155**: Background: ©Gary Bell/OceanwideImages.com **pp. 156-157**: Bottom row, left to right: ©Krzysztof Odziomek/Shutterstock.com; ©Teguh Tirtaputra/Shutterstock.com; ©pitcharee/Shutterstock.com; ©Silke Baron/Shutterstock.com; ©Tony Wear/Shutterstock.com **p. 156**: ©David Shen/Seapics.com **p. 157**: ©Hungarian Snow/Creative Commons Attribution-Share Alike 2.0 Generic license **pp. 158-159**: ©Marty Snyderman; Bottom row, left to right: ©Darryl Brooks/Shutterstock.com; ©BW Folsom/Shutterstock.com; ©Photobar/Shutterstock.com; ©Discovery Channel/Chris Fallows; ©Willtu/Dreamstime.com; ©Snaprender/Shutterstock.com **pp. 160-161**: Background: ©Discovery Channel/Jackie Forster **p. 160**: Discover Channel/Chris Fallows **p. 161**: bottom, left to right: tratong/Shutterstock.com; ©Colin Edwards Photography/Shutterstock.com; ©Eric Isselee/Shutterstock.com **pp. 162-163**: Background, top right, bottom right: ©Discovery

Channel/Chris Fallows **p. 162**: ©Ethan Daniels **p. 164**: Background: ©KatAlekStudio/Shutterstock.com; Left: GNU Free Documentation License; Right: ©Hawaii Shark Encounters **p. 165**: Top: ©Discovery Channel/Cameron Davidson; Second row left center, and right: ©Discovery Channel; Third row left: ©Carsten Medom Madsen/Shutterstock.com; Third row right: ©Ivan Cholakov/Shutterstock.com; ©Bottom row left: ©Sushkin/Shutterstock.com; Bottom right: ©Jun Xiao /Shutterstock.com **pp. 166-167**: Background: ©Andy Murch/OceanwideImages.com **p. 167**: ©apomares/istockphoto.com **pp. 168-169**: Discovery Channel **p. 170**: Left: ©Discovery Channel/Ian Cartwright; Right: ©Prisma/SuperStock **p. 171**: Top: ©Andy Murch/OceanwideImages.com; Bottom: ©Matthieu Godbout/GNU Free Documentation License; Right©delacy/Shutterstock.com

**SHARK BITES**
**pp. 172-173**: Background: ©littlesam/Shutterstock.com **p. 172**: Top ©Eduard Hladky/Shutterstock.com; Center: ©U.S. Navy; Bottom: ©Ciurzynski/Shutterstock.com **p. 173**: Top left: ©Gustavo Miguel Fernandes/Shutterstock.com; Bottom left: ©A Cotton Photo/Shutterstock.com **pp. 174-175**: Background: ©Strejman/Shutterstock.com Top: ©Vitoriano Junior/Shutterstock.com Bottom left: ©Ian Woolcock/Shutterstock.com Bottom right: ©Pipop Boosarakumwadi/Shutterstock.com **p. 175**: Top to bottom: ©infografick/Shutterstock.com; ©Janelle Lugge/Shutterstock.com; ©Gary Saxe/Shutterstock.com; ©Ruth Peterkin/Shutterstock.com; ©Bob Reynolds/Shutterstock.com **pp. 176-177**: Background: ©Library of Congress **p. 176**: Top: ©Library of Congress; Center: ©KMusser/GNU Free Documentation License; Bottom: ©Jim Gore/Jim Gore Antiques, Cream Ridge, NJ **p. 177**: Top left:

©cdelay/Shutterstock.com; Bottom left: ©Shane Gross/Shutterstock.com **pp. 178-179**: Background: ©littlesam/Shutterstock.com **p. 179**: Left: ©Rihardzz/Shutterstock.com; Right: © Image Source/SuperStock **pp. 180-181**: Background: ©littlesam **p. 180**: Left: ©Gwen Lowe/Seapics.com; Right: ©Discovery Channel/C. Copeman: **p. 181**: Top left: ©AP Photos/Paul Sakuma; Bottom left: ©AP Photo/Monterey County Herald/David Royal; Right: ©Discovery Channel/Sunshine Beach Photos

**SAWSHARKS**
**pp. 182-183**: ©Marty Snyderman **pp. 184-185**: Background: ©Rudy Kuiter/OceanwideImages.com **p. 184**: Top: ©Image Source/SuperStock; Bottom: age ©fotostock/SuperStock **p. 185**: ©Marty Snyderman

**NEW SHARKS**
**pp. 186-187**: ©Discovery Channel **p. 186**: ©California Academy of Sciences

## ACKNOWLEDGMENTS

We'd like to thank the following people who helped in the creation of this book:

Meri Bell
Peg Cook
Sue Dabritz
Clara Favale-Borys
Tori Gilbert
Patrick Knopf Insinger
Susan Sojourner Insinger
Alexandra Israel
Steve Kaufman
Ana Leal
Devin O'Connor
J. T. O'Connor
Dr. Jack Randall
Tom Sheeter
Deena Stein
Michelle Stein
Bonnie Lane Webber